DIAL M
FOR MERTHYR

On Tour with Midasuno
****king, ***king & ****ting

Rachel Trezise was born in the Rhondda Valley in 1978. She studied at Glamorgan and Limerick Universities. Her first novel *In and Out of the Goldfish Bowl* was a winner of the Orange Futures Prize. Her first collection of short fiction *Fresh Apples* won the EDS Dylan Thomas Prize. She is currently working on her second novel.

There's no one writing such gritty, personal, ballsy literature ... She manages to completely strip away the myth.

Scott Andrews

An outstanding young writer

The Times

The arrival of a major new literary talent

Mario Basini

Laugh Out Loud Funny

Peter Florence

DIAL M
FOR MERTHYR

On Tour with Midasuno
****king, ***king & ****ting

Rachel Trezise

PARTHIAN

Parthian
The Old Surgery
Napier Street
Cardigan
SA43 1ED

www.parthianbooks.co.uk

First published in 2007
© Rachel Trezise 2007
All Rights Reserved

ISBN 978-1-905762-12-5

Edited by Gwen Davies & Jeni Williams

Cover design & typesetting by Lucy Llewellyn
Printed and bound by Gomer, Llandysul, Wales

The publisher acknowledges the financial support of
the Welsh Books Council.

British Library Cataloguing in Publication Data

A cataloguing record for this book is available from
the British Library.

To my brother Preston

The music business is a cruel and shallow money trench; a long plastic hallway where thieves and pimps run free and good men die like dogs. There's also a negative side.

Hunter S Thompson

PART ONE

PART ONE

In The Beginning

It was 1978, July, a Sunday, when I was born in my parent's bedroom. My father was a carpenter that year. My mother wore paisley blouses with enormous collars – in the sepia photographs she looks like a thirteen-year-old boy. Cwmparc, their tiny village in the Rhondda Valley, had dried up under the heat wave. There were no puddles in the cracked pavements and wasting water was banned. It was five years since Max Boyce recorded *Live at Treorchy*, and my grandmother's wicked cackle was immortalised on vinyl. (One English journalist mistakenly read the title as 'Living in Treachery.') Wales had won the Grand Slam in the spring. I imagine the pig's head-shaped country with a red and white striped scarf swathed around it. In the bedroom next door my ten-year-old brother had turned the volume up on his clunky tape recorder, trying to drown out my mother's excruciating, childbearing shrieks. He was playing punk music.

As a toddler, the guttural rumpus of the Sex Pistols came simply to be the sound of the record player in the living room. I was about four when my father disappeared and my mother started working three jobs to pay the mortgage. My brother had a big, red drum-kit in the middle of the room and a big group of friends with tight jeans and Mohicans. One of them had a guitar. In the evenings we'd all sit around listening to *Never Mind The Bollocks* and *London Calling*, ignoring the neighbours rapping on the glass of the front window. They had *The Great Rock 'n' Roll Swindle* on video and we'd keep rewinding it to the part where Sid Vicious came out in his bondage trousers and white dinner jacket and shot all the audience members in cold blood, before he sang 'My Way', a wonderful, impious snarl on his mouth. Either that or we'd watch the snuff movie where the Chinese gangster cut the girl's hand off and her fingers kept moving. In infant school one afternoon, I closed my colourful text book and stood up on my little plastic chair. I was wearing my red dress with the lace frills around the neckline. 'Listen to this song I've learnt,' I said to the teacher. She sat back in her chair, nodding to the class; silently asking them for their patience, most likely expecting a nursery rhyme. 'It was on the good ship Venus,' I sang. 'By Christ, ya shoulda seen us, the figure head was a whore in bed and the mast, a mammoth penis.' I was taken to the Headmistress's office where I was allowed to sing the rest of 'Friggin' in the Riggin' and my mother turned up fretting quarter of an hour later. Of course to most people punk was a murky world of heroin abuse and violence. Four months after I was born Sid Vicious had been arrested for stabbing his girlfriend, Nancy Spungen, in Manhattan's Chelsea Hotel, and then he'd OD'd. For me it was merely the sound of my brother. He was a fifteen-year-old boy. I was a five-year-old girl. Conversation was awkward. I came to know him by the music he chose to express himself with. The Sex Pistols were the angry soundtrack to the life of a distressed teenager. Easily, I came to understand that the music you chose to play was the voice you were giving to your otherwise silent soul.

My mother kept playing country & western music. She had an album cover propped up on her dressing table, a picture of the most glamorous woman I'd ever seen, with a mound of platinum blonde curls, long, blue eyelashes and an impossible chest. I was most obsessed by her Cinderella slippers, high heels propped up onto a chaise longue with a pom-pom of purple ostrich feathers on either toe. I used to sneak into my mother's room merely to stare at her, as though she was some kind of fairy, an oddity who could vanish as quickly as my father did. With age I came to discover that it was Dolly Parton. And I gradually began to decipher what was hiding behind her soft guitar chords and kooky, breathy inflection. Her songs sounded like fluttering, effortless ditties but the lyrics were all about failed love affairs, domestic abuse, prostitution and the abhorrence of working a 9 to 5. My mother would sit in front of her mirror in her black lace balconette bra, trowelling her mascara on with a kohl-crusty make-up brush, happily humming 'Fancy', a Bobby Gentry song about an eighteen-year-old New Orleans girl whose mother made her sell her body to buy food for her baby sister because her father'd run off with the cash, or 'Jolene', a song about insecurity and sexual jealousy, or 'Ode To Billy Joe', a song about suicide and bereavement. Country music was miserable, and I came to understand, as I had with my brother, that when my mother played her music she was

5

wallowing in the sadness of a lonely divorcee; metaphorically, and often physically sobbing into her sherry about the men she'd loved and lost, the children she had to bring up single-handedly, and all manner of complicated grown-up women's things.

Sitting on some pigeon hole reference system, dead centre between punk with its DIY brashness, and country with its calm melancholy, is rock music – a broad genus which takes in everything from the Rolling Stones to Metallica. I discovered it in 1990, a couple of years after the release of *Appetite for Destruction* in the US. It was still early enough to witness the exhilarating worldwide explosion of Guns 'n' Roses, the band that had made it. I was twelve and dangerously close to puberty. I'd started practising my French kissing technique on my pillowcase, started touching myself intimately. But in my imagination, the face underneath me and the fingers hovering around my pelvic bone belonged to bass player Duff McKagan. Here was a peroxide blonde in a torn CBGB T-shirt, defined, tattooed, sweat-coated arms plucking a guitar slung down at his skinny knees, his sneering, obliging mouth roaring Misfits lyrics into a microphone, a black Stetson on his head. At last I'd found the echo of my spirit – a sexy, thundering clamour that would come to encompass my heartaches, my angst, my esteem, my tribulations, my joy, my*self*.

One year later, after three weeks sleeping on the pavements of Nottingham city and stealing into the shower room at the leisure centre to wash, I'd found a squat in the centre of the red light region. It was the first bath I'd had in a month. I lay back in the tepid water, staring blankly at the black and white chequered tiles, the cold bombarding through a smash-hole in the windowpane. Bon Jovi's eagerly awaited new album *Keep the Faith* had been released at the beginning of the week. I could hear it vaguely through the walls and I played at guessing which bedsit it came from. There were two men on the ground floor. One was a German taxi driver with unusually large ears, the other was Sam, a cook who worked at the café where I was a newly employed waitress, his feet permanently planted into the scabbards of neon pink cowboy boots. I stretched out of the water to pick up the paperback he'd loaned me.

It was Thursday. The city was easing into the weekend. The girls lined the Boulevard, one hovering around the stem of every concrete lamppost, in their PVC, track-marks scoring their arms, stilettos clicking. They watched me vigilantly, checking that I didn't stop inside their patch – a fresh-faced fourteen-year-old, it had to be bad for business. Near the university I saw Kris on his way home from the afternoon shift, his indigo braids tied up in a bandana, protected from the stink of chip fat. He waved but disappeared among the customers weaving around the maze of pubs on Parliament Street. Martha & the Muffins' 'Echo Beach' was spiralling out of the fire-exit of a wine-bar. I tried not to think of my brother – I might not ever see him again.

My Swedish blagging partner, Camilla, had found digs with a boyfriend in Ilkeston. She needed to marry someone for a visa. She'd already hitched a lift to Rock City; she was fourth in the queue of leather jackets, smiling with buck teeth, her purple hair extensions landing on a ripped Skid Row T-shirt. She'd learned her art in London where she'd spend whole days sitting on the floor of the city airport, begging tourists for the last of their useless sterling. I got the feeling she enjoyed it.

7

A million quid wouldn't be enough to stop her holding a paper coffee cup to the sky and I was hoping some of her recklessness would rub off on me. I was on the run; earnestly trying to scurry away from a crap childhood. We pooled our coins and paid the entrance fee. It was unsigned night but the band hadn't started. The DJ was playing *The A-Team* theme tune. I was at the bar trying to order lemonade and ready salted crisps. The files of punters around me were mostly wearing black velvet leggings with frilly white shirts. The men had leather waistcoats. Jet, a character from the ITV show *Gladiators*, was dancing seductively against the balcony railings and everyone's necks were craned up, watching her. Suddenly Mad Dog materialised, two empty plastic tumblers in his hands. 'Ay op duck, ya orright?' He was the resident caretaker, a man with strawberry blonde spikes, the same shape and length as Vivian's from *The Young Ones*. I actually remember him as having three silver stars studded into his forehead, although he probably didn't. As a sideline he'd make a pretence of washing the plate glass windows of the city at half-past seven in the morning – just as my shift was about to finish. A bucket of sullied water splashing against the café façade was my cue to leave. I smiled at him.

'Ya comin' in cubby for a drink?' he said. 'C'mon.' He had his own staff room at the back of the club, a walk-in cupboard cramped with cleaning paraphernalia. Somehow he'd managed to squeeze a plastic beer-garden table in there and he'd sit at it all night, smoking pot. I followed him to his lair, prising my caffeine tablets out of my handbag. Seeing him had reminded me of work. My shift started in three hours. He opened the door and sent me in first. Quite astoundingly, Alice Cooper was in there, sitting amongst the mop handles. I stared at the black face-paint swathed in diamond shapes around his blue eyes. The corners bled down his jowls in rivulets, like oily tears. Mad Dog pushed by me and opened the bottle of Jack Daniels on the table between them. The feature film *Wayne's World* had been released earlier that year and I couldn't get the scene out of my head where Mike Myers and Dana Carvey, challenged with the same predicament, bowed before him chanting, 'We're not worthy, we're not worthy.' I sat on an upside-down beer crate. Mad Dog was pouring the whiskey. It smelt like sweet and sour sick. He passed me his plastic tumbler for a taste. I sipped it carefully, holding the fiery liquid on my tongue for as long as I possibly could. 'C'mon on then mate,' Mad Dog said, slapping Alice Cooper on the sleeve of his leather coat. 'He was just telling me all about Elvis.'

'Elvis?' Alice Cooper said, 'Gee, Elvis, yeah, it was Memphis, 1962...'

Because of his hit, 'School's Out', I was thinking about my maths teacher. She'd wiped the floor with me at the start of term in September because I hadn't shown the workings-out on my summer homework. Completing an equation of that magnitude in one step would make me a mathematician, she said, and that was at the very least, unlikely. If only she could have seen me now. Did it look like I gave a flying fuck about equations? After work that morning, I watched the news on the portable in the taxi rank behind the café. Thatcher was ordering the closure of every coal mine in Wales. I took my £20 wage to the Quasar Centre on Maid Marian Way. It was a kind of indoor paint-balling arena with laser guns instead of paint bombs – the most fun thing you could do with your clothes on, or, if like me you were jailbait, the most fun thing full stop. It was £7 for forty-five minutes.

When I got back to the bedsit in North Sherwood, Kris was shading his eyes from the daylight pouring through the gap in the black curtain. A drawing pin had worked its way out of the rotting window frame. His skinny legs were tangled in the grubby sheets of his antique bed. 'Is it tomorrow already?' he said. He sat up and put his jeans on. I undressed and fell into the warm patch he'd left in the malodorous mattress. There were dents where his bony knees had been. We did alternate shifts at the café and alternate shifts in his bed. It was my greatest fear, and simultaneously my most rousing fantasy, that one day he wouldn't go to work. We'd spend all day together in his filthy room, lying on his creaking bed frame. He watched me for a moment from the doorway. 'Night then, Welsh girl,' he said and he turned the broken handle.

Troedyrhiw

It was October 1992. Back in the South Wales Valleys, my mother was turning frantic. She did an interview with the local newspaper, pleading for my safe return. COME HOME RACHEL, the front page headline said in inch-high bold black letters, a photograph of me wearing a Batman T-shirt in the top right hand corner. I had no way of seeing that request because the *Rhondda Leader* circulated only in the Rhondda. It was a thrilling but ultimately ineffective cut of local news, an antecedent to the 'Look Who's Been in Court' columns; prime gossip fodder. Months later I'd scissor the story out of its border of adverts and mount it on my bedroom wall, impressed by my own anarchism. At the time, one of the Guns 'n' Roses music videos, rotated regularly on MTV, featured a childhood mug shot of Duff McKagan printed on the side of a milk carton. Maybe it was this image, branded on my spongy brain, which made me think of my own circumstance as some sort of passport to insubordination. I was one of them now; the famous, the lawless, the sexy, and nothing was going to restrain me.

The story was old news when I found it beneath the cotton reels in my mother's sewing cupboard. It was forgotten amidst the television footage from Westminster of Margaret Thatcher declaring the end of the industrial age, the handles of her handbag propped ridiculously on her forearm; the final nail in the coffin of British proletarian livelihoods. Subsequently, the Welsh news introduced interviews with defiant NUM leaders, hell bent on fighting the closures. There was only one working coal mine left in Wales by now, the Tower Colliery in Hirwaun, near Aberdare, and the workers were forming a syndicate to buy it, sure that they could continue to make a living digging coal. The jury was out but nobody really expected the scheme to be a success. South Wales, as a nation, had become adept at not expecting very much.

Tower sat halfway between me and Troedyrhiw, a small village in the Merthyr Valley, a fifteen-minute drive from the actual town; fifteen miles from Treorchy, as the crow flies. In the 1700s it was the home of the Plymouth Ironworks and Colliery, part of the renowned Cyfarthfa Ironworks. The stone sleepers of Richard Trevithick's first railway journey could still be traced along the village pathways, beneath the shadow of Aberfan cemetery, looming perpetually on the adjacent mountainside. Matt Riste, born in Merthyr General Hospital in 1983, had lived in the same house, in the same area, for the full nine years of his life, listening to his elder sister Martine play Bon Jovi records in her bedroom. They weren't close – they were aged too far apart – but that music infiltrated Matt's consciousness. There was no such thing as pop culture in

Merthyr, not a visible one, not at nine years old. Life was about going to school and getting home and going to school again; doing what you needed to do. Music, of any description, was an organic experience, spurred inadvertently through the tastes of family members. Bon Jovi were the fundamental order of the day, made so by their worldwide chart success throughout the latter half of the eighties. Their second album, *Slippery When Wet*, released in 1986, would become one of the six top-selling rock albums of all time. I clearly remember being sent by my mother to deliver a grocery bag of gifts to my detested cousins who lived a few terraces away. It was Christmas Eve and I was eight. I walked quickly, scanning the cold, grey pavement and the Santa Claus motifs on the thin silver wrapping paper, singing the chorus to 'Livin' on a Prayer' at the top of my voice, as though it was indeed a prayer which could somehow reverse my reluctance. That song was everywhere, on the radio in my brother's garage, the television at my Nanna's house, in the headphones of my babysitter's Walkman. It surrounded me like family. I didn't know it then, but it suited the jukeboxes of Wales because its lyrics about the struggles of blue collar workers in New Jersey (the band's industrialised homestate) also portrayed life here. But the song's most redeeming feature was its ability to glamorise the working class plight; to turn poverty into romance, survival into courage, workaday into theatre; to make us feel as if we were alive. The cover of the album included a photograph of a throng of big-busted, bikinied blondes washing the body of a sports car with foaming chamois. At the height of eighties Conservatism it was a moderately risqué image, and not a little attractive, which is why, when it was released here, the picture got moved from the cover to the inside sleeve.

In the summer, Martine married Vince, another rock fan. Vince had an extensive record collection and he put it immediately to use; recording mix cassettes for his nine-year-old brother-in-law. Matt listened to the songs with his friend, Scott Andrews. He too, had lived in Troedyrhiw all his life. They'd been friends since they met at nursery school. There was a lot going on in the world of rock music in the early nineties (namely, its own death, but nobody who actually liked rock music realised this at the time) and there was a lot going on on those tapes, most notably Metallica and Guns 'n' Roses. Both bands were created as antidotes to the glam scene, prevalent since Bon Jovi's success. Their ethos was to focus on the music they were playing as opposed to the cosmetics they were wearing. Each boy claimed a band for himself. Metallica was Matt's, Guns 'n' Roses was Scott's, and in order to quench their new-found thirst for rock music, they pursued it in the pages of *Kerrang!* which they collected religiously, and on MTV's *Headbanger's Ball*. (It was televised at midnight on a Sunday, a school night – Matt set his alarm to skulk downstairs and record it.) From their physical world, an employment black spot, they looked to a mental one; a pornography of money, fame, liberty and domination, all for no reason outside itself, and all based in the magic of music. The very notion of rock 'n' roll fuelled them onto comprehensive school and lunchtime drum lessons practising paradiddles on the desk lids for months, never getting close to a real kit.

The Naval Club

When I think about my time at comprehensive school, what I remember most vividly is the last two years, and most specifically, non-uniform day. On the last Friday before the Easter holidays the pupils would pay 50p into the Comic Relief fund and in return were able to wear their own clothes. This was a great opportunity for me to parade to lessons in my new coat. It was a black leather biker jacket with the red Skid Row emblem decorating the tail band. I'd paid a student from the art college to painstakingly reproduce every character with acrylic paint. I had also achieved my lifelong ambition of getting my nose pierced by walking into a Nottingham bazaar and insisting I was sixteen, shortly before the police picked me up and drove me back to the Rhondda. It was against the rules to wear any kind of jewellery to school and I kept the hole in my nostril open by sawing the gems from the top of studs and simply keeping the hypoallergenic trunk in the hole. Sometimes this would push itself up to the surface and jump of its own accord onto the essay I was writing or into the breakfast cereal I was eating. Keeping all of my little fashion adornments hidden away was becoming problematic and non-uniform day, save for weekends, was the only day of the year I didn't have to. Instead of my navy A-line skirt and school tie, I strode to class wearing my drainpipe jeans and Dr Martens, studded wristbands snaking up my forearms. A thick silver chain linked my nose-ring to my earring. I was proud of my rock music inspired identity and wanted to thrust it in the face of authority.

But it wasn't the teachers who objected to my dress; curiously it was the other kids. Nobody had heard of Skid Row. The mainstream British Top Twenty was crammed full of boy bands – clean cut drama students who didn't know what a musical instrument looked like. All they had to do was turn up, mime and dance and look pretty. Their songs were written by invisible producers – manufactured pop music designed for maximum consumption; buy it, use it, throw it away. Real music was distinctly unfashionable and Cwmparc, insular, small town that it was, did not encourage sub-cultures. Kids in brand name sports clothes who danced on Friday evenings at the youth club to computer generated drum-beats voiced their opposition mostly with petty name-calling. Occasionally, a fourteen-year-old boy would punch me covertly in the midriff as he passed. It taught me a valuable lesson – nearly all of the world's population had appalling taste and dismal though it was, they'd go to violent lengths to protect it. I left school in 1994 and went home to dye my hair blue. I was living on my own in a terraced house on the main road. My brother had long since shaped his own life. My mother had virtually moved in with one of her boyfriends. I spent most of my time with my face buried in the pages of *Kerrang!* dreaming about flying to LA and doing filthy things with Duff McKagan. The only practical things I ever attempted were colourful charcoal sketches of electric guitars. I enrolled to study my A Levels at the local college. The art department called me back to school, imploring me to go on to sixth form, but I'd already set fire to my tie.

On returning to the Rhondda two years earlier I'd discovered the valley had its own kind of Rock City: a lopsided building, obscured by fly posters, standing on the top of Tonypandy Square. It was called The Naval Club. It had the words 'All Hippies Smell' scratched into its grand wooden doors. I went there every Saturday wearing denim hot-pants, drinking snake-bite and blackcurrant and got a lift home with the man who managed the burger van outside; I used to lean on the worktop, filching the processed cheese slices out of their cellophane covers. It was here, one night, that I realised music could be made by ordinary people. A local band was on the stage playing a metal cover of the theme tune to the children's programme *Rainbow*. The singer spoke between songs with a valley accent, almost identical to my own. The DIY ethic the Sex Pistols had been preaching in the room next-door to my delivery couldn't have ever really penetrated my consciousness because I thought all singers spoke with west coast American accents, or at the very least, English ones. I had apparently assumed that CDs fell out of the sky – already neatly packaged. It was a strange and comforting revelation. Music however, had changed. Guns 'n' Roses split up to the tune of ten-minute piano ballads, Axl Rose absorbed by his own ego, Duff McKagan bloated by alcoholism. Glam rock, hard rock, heavy metal; it disappeared overnight. Grunge, a phenomenon created in Seattle by a melting pot of rain, coffee and depression, moved quickly into the limelight. It was the soundtrack to Northwest Noir; a pungent guitar din punctuated by angst. Rock stars weren't decadent anymore. They didn't wear cowboy boots anymore. They came in a standard uniform of ripped jeans and chequered shirts. Pop culture had turned wretched and romantic, wallowing in its own hedonism. It had eaten itself.

I was fifteen when I fell in love. I met my boyfriend at the Naval. He was eighteen and celestial, an art student from the local college with long, chocolate brown hair and muscled thighs. He had a pet iguana and played guitar in a rock band. He lived in a tiny flat in Maerdy with his mother and brothers. We used to sit on his bunk, kissing, slowly delving deeper into one another's bodies, lingering on the easy pleasure of touch. On New Year night we got hold of a bottle of whiskey and went all the way – a big tsunami of sex; my first orgasm. The band was called Accidental Genocide – a thrash five-piece who played Iron Maiden and Metallica covers. Most of them had mullets and wore black drainpipe jeans with white, big-tongued trainers. The chubby frontman sang falsetto, holding his microphone above his face, his legs spread defiantly. They looked like a circus act. It was 1994 after all, the year Kurt Cobain blew his brains out. Everyone was wearing smiley-faced Nirvana T-shirts, even kids who'd been at school with me. Youth culture had adopted a new lifestyle. Nobody took speed or cocaine anymore. Drugs of choice were Prozac, pot and in extreme cases, heroin. Nobody could listen to 80mph flying V riffs on downers. Nobody wanted to. But the band continued rehearsing. They couldn't get any local gigs because

18

everyone knew how awful they were. I travelled with them around the country, loading amplifiers into rock clubs only to load them out again when they were paid off in the half-time break. Their one redeeming feature was my boyfriend. He was the youngest and most talented member. I was sure he'd be better off without them so I secretly sent copies of his demo to record companies and purposely made him late for everything; tempting him back to bed on a Sunday afternoon when he should have been at practice. The band members began to suspect I was a Yoko Ono character, snatching their John Lennon away. Their girlfriends were late twenty-something hairdressers in twin sets who baulked at my hair dye and fishnet stockings. I didn't fit into their neat little knitting circle. Within a year my adoration for my boyfriend very steadily turned into a debilitating obsession, a hysteria which caused me to try and strangle him during sex. I also tried to bite his tongue off and put his favourite guitar in a hot and bubbly bath. Neurosis got the better of us after eighteen months and I left him for another, not so talented, guitarist. The Naval Club closed down. Accidental Genocide gave up.

I started to cut my arms following the break up with my boyfriend; maybe it was triggered by guilt. I believed I had disturbed the hands of fate and that my life would suffer eternally so I began work on a slow and painful suicide, lying in the bath scoring welts into my skin with a razor blade. It was intended as punishment but it turned very quickly into relief. The blood assured me that I was still alive. It was like having a piss when I'd been yearning for hours to go. At the same time I started stealing pills out of my mother's Valium prescription, chalky blue 10mls that turned me into a walking

19

zombie. When my mother realised what I was doing she stopped paying my pocket money and gave me pills to sell instead. There was a drug-house close to the local pub and I'd go there to exchange the Diazepam for cash.

There was always a group of men sitting around on the tatty sofa in the tiny living room, rolling joints, watching pirate videos. One of the films they watched was Oliver Stone's *Natural Born Killers*, a story of two victims of traumatised childhoods who became lovers and psychopathic murderers, irresponsibly glorified by the media. What I noticed immediately was that the film had an incredible soundtrack. Part way through their depraved killing spree, Mickey and Mallory Knox found themselves in a New Mexico desert, quarrelling over Mickey's new-found fondness for female hostages. There is a magnificently haunting track scored across the scene; a sparse and throbbing melody under which a man whispers the resonant lyrics. It's called 'Something I Can Never Have'. The punch-line, 'Everywhere I look you're all I see, just a fading fucking reminder of who I used to be', was tailor-made for my heart-break, and the something I could never have was an untainted sanity. The song guided me quickly to Trent Reznor, the film's music compiler and sole member of American synthesizer band, Nine Inch Nails. He was a wan, dark-haired man in black leather who used the heel of his dominatrix-style boots to kick the life out of pianos and snap microphone stands to bits. His debut album, *Pretty Hate Machine*, had been released five years earlier and went triple platinum in the US, possibly because it vocalised the quiet violence and teenage angst prevalent in anyone at school-leaving age. It was an anthology of lyrical hostilities regarding lust and futile relationships; growing pains set to piercing riffs and acidic drum-machine-beats. Its tone snared me with despairing rapture. I thought he'd written those songs for me.

In 1994 I was watching MTV with the sound turned down. I don't remember where I was exactly but I think it was a waiting room in a dentist surgery because the memory comes back with toothache. I only went there when I urgently needed treatment and I had two molars taken out that year, casualties of my most non-toxic addiction, chocolate. The image on the screen was of a flame-haired girl sitting at a baby grand. A minute or so into the video rats materialised at the keys and crawled up her bare arms and neck. I was enamoured with this picture because I had a pet rat of my own, an albino called Snowball who I carried around in my coat pocket. I nodded at the screen, approving of the image. After a while I became frustrated about not being able to hear the music that she was playing and scanned the faces around me for similar sentiments, only to be met with indifference. At the end of the video I made a mental note of her name; Tori Amos. She was a part-Scottish, part-Cherokee American, daughter of a Presbyterian priest who grew up playing piano in church. She was the youngest person ever to get a scholarship to the Peabody Conservatory of Music only to be expelled in her early teens because of the growing influence of popular music on her work. She'd go on to play gay piano bars in Baltimore City, chaperoned by her father. Later she moved to Los Angeles to pursue her career, continuing to play bars. One night, she gave a patron a lift home and he raped her. I procured a copy of her 1992 debut, *Little Earthquakes,* and put it in my bedroom CD player. It was a delicate progressive rock work that used piano like a guitar, immediately listenable and challenging. Its intimacy was uncompromising and

21

intense, her lyrics encompassing defiance, sarcasm and rage. There was a song on there called 'Me and a Gun', stripped of all music save for Amos' voice, which confronted me with the story of her rape. She said that while she was being molested she thought about Barbados – she had to survive because she'd never been to Barbados. I laughed out loud at the truth in her words. More than that, I was struck by 'Silent All These Years', the protagonist of which was a shy, young girl, hearing her voice for the first time: 'Years go by, will I choke on my tears 'til finally there's nothing left, one more casualty, you know we're too easy, easy, easy.' It was reminiscent of the very secret experience I had caged up in the back of my head, the thing which was making me self-destruct. I know that she wrote that song for me and it made me want to open the window and let out an acute primal scream. What I wanted to say precisely I wasn't sure, but I was certain I wanted to be heard. At the very least it made me want to write poetry.

These two performers would shortly go on to find one another. Trent Reznor collaborated with Tori Amos on 'Past the Mission', a song from her second album. They'd record it in the former LA house of Roman Polanski where Reznor had built a studio to record *The Downward Spiral*, placing the control box in the room where Manson butchered Sharon Tate. They were musicians who taught me as much about communication as Maya Angelou and Toni Morrison, authors whose books I was studying for A Level. For a while I assumed I, like them, should be addressing my story with music. I knew a few guitar chords so I joined a local industrial band called Shatner. The previous member's speciality had been an ability to sing in an Icelandic accent, like Björk. I didn't get to write anything. The bassist gave me a lyric sheet to learn, sixth form verse with song titles like 'Brain Tumour Blues' and 'Spastic's Day Out'. The Thursday night rehearsals had more to do with an age-old competition the other members had of cooking curry with the most inappropriate ingredients than they did with musical creativity. In the last one I went to, the bassist had included a pair of his mother's soiled knickers.

My narrative was obviously something I'd need to write alone. I left the music out altogether. The 'Silent All These Years' refrain became the opening words of my debut novel, five years later.

Opium Dens

Gavin Jessop was thirteen years old when he found himself in South Wales. Born in Penzance, Cornwall, on his mother's 1983 tour of Navy duty, he was brought up in a single parent family in Llanelli, west Wales. In 1996, his mother married a man from Troedyrhiw and he moved contentedly into the village. Post-industrial Merthyr, where fly-by-night factories had replaced mines and ironworks and TV and pop music had swept away chapel religion, was stimulating after twelve years living in a farming community. It took a trend two years on average to move from Cardiff into the Valleys but around seven to reach Llanelli. Guitar music was an unknown entity. He listened, like all the other thirteen-year-olds in his native west Wales, to dance music borne by the mainstream Ecstasy-fuelled club culture. He also played football, and every season attended the local trophy presentation. There, for some reason, girls always let him kiss them. He was attempting to break his current record (eighteen in one night), when he met another thirteen-year-old footballer. His name was Scott Andrews. Scott liked rock music. He wanted to be in a rock band. He loved Guns 'n' Roses, and would look at each member in awe; Axl Rose, the kilt-wearing, red-headed, raw-throat singer, Slash, the black, big curly-haired, top hat, topless axeman, Izzy Stradlin, the New York Dolls styled rhythm guitarist and Duff McKagan, the peroxide bassist punk. They were all cool. The only one he *didn't* want to look like was the drummer. There was a purple BC Rich bass guitar with silver lightning forks painted down its sides, hanging in the window of Merthyr Sounds. Scott was saving up to buy it when his parents got him an amplifier and Stratocaster for Christmas, automatically limiting his choice to guitarist. Gavin's brother-in-law, a man who wore a bandana stuffed in his denim arse pocket, and who therefore reminded Scott of Slash, gradually taught him how to play it. Gavin succumbed to his own rock 'n' roll fate meanwhile, when Scott, having tried to impress his tastes on the new boy by lending him tapes he'd rarely bother listening to, hit the jackpot with an Offspring album.

Matt Riste was indifferent to his education. Afon Taff High School was a routine he practised; he listened in class, he put his homework in on time. He was an average pupil who managed to avoid bullying because he was big. Living in Merthyr was something he accepted, because he'd never been anywhere else. But aged thirteen he was already dreaming of escape. Every evening after school, Scott went back to Matt's house where he'd try to figure the tablature for Nirvana's 'Smells Like Teen Spirit' out on his guitar. When they weren't thinking about their embryonic band, The New Roses, they thought about joining the Army, or the Navy. For two years in a row they spent their long summer holidays manufacturing dens draped in sheets of camouflage. On a bank holiday in 1997, only notes away from completing the song, Scott threw his guitar aside and suggested they attend the Army Open Day in nearby Garw Nant, which they did, whiling the afternoon away riding on tanks. Matt soon discovered that Scott already played in a band, albeit The Hot Rats, a cover cabaret act, their line-up concluded by Gavin Jessop on bass. Matt's jealousy drove him home to his parents, where he demanded an authentic drum kit; actual drums, genuine drumsticks – it was time to really learn to play.

Aged fourteen, Scott, Matt and Gavin were four years into comprehensive school and the 'rock kids' naturally gravitated towards each other. Steven Hopkins, a boy Scott had befriended earlier in the year when they both turned up to PE wearing the same Manic Street Preachers T-shirt, and another boy, Michael, became bona fide members of a private music club. They were sitting in a science lesson one afternoon, aimlessly toying with the Bunsen burner gas tap in the centre of the wooden work bench when they vowed to start a band together. They christened it 'Opium' there and then. The Hot Rats having disintegrated somewhere down the line, the five piece immediately began rehearsals in Matt's parents' garage. They sound-proofed the walls with egg boxes, an ultimately pointless measure – complaints from the neighbours were frequent. Every weekend they'd sleep in the garage, shivering the night away on the concrete floor. Weekends turned to weekdays, and they practically moved into the garage, walking to school and back again in their uniforms. It was around eighteen months, a period containing two snowy winters, before they were confident enough for their first live gig – a birthday party in a friend's living room. The long hours paid off. It was a success and through friends of friends of friends, paid pub gigs began arriving. A few months later however, a few weeks into a new year, Scott began complaining about the heavily laden line-up. Including him as a frontman there were three guitarists competing for lead. With Steven Hopkins having learned the compositions more quickly and skilfully than Michael, the obvious solution was to let the latter go. It was left to Matt to tell him he was sacked.

It was a January morning, frost thick on the pavement, and Matt and Michael were walking reluctantly to school. Michael was excited by an upcoming gig; chattering rapidly about which band T-shirt he was going to wear. Matt listened for a while, staring at the frozen leaves dotted along the path, before he interrupted. Only a few weeks previously, Michael's parents had bought him an amplifier, a guitar, two new pedals and a guitar strap for Christmas, pleased that their seemingly apathetic son had found a hobby. Michael stared disbelievingly at Matt for a few seconds before turning and running away. They'd never speak again. Disillusioned, Matt put Opium on the back burner and concentrated on his school-leaving job at Poundstretcher in Pentrebach. He stocked the shelves of the bargain basement with dirt cheap clothes and bric-a-brac, and it would be another year before Scott rang Matt on Boxing Day 1999 and played a song he'd written down the telephone line. He was calling it 'The Art of Fear'. Two years after that, it would become Midasuno's first single.

On The Dole

The walls of the make-shift classroom were painted magnolia. The other kids were younger than me, boys in their late teens wearing thick, gold belcher chains, boys who had never gone to school. The tutor was a patient man who stood in front of the blackboard affecting a telephone manner while his students aimed biros at the market traders on the street below us, shouting, 'Pakis, fuck off.' It was 2001 and I'd been on the dole for twelve months. I was trying to write a book based on a fantasy about fucking Kelly Jones when the people at the benefits office sent me on a fortnight training course. Its purpose, they said, was to teach me to write a curriculum vitae; a flagrant insult. I had an degree in English and a best-selling autobiographical novel. 'I'm a writer,' I said. 'I know how to knock up a CV.' The civil servant simply smirked at me from behind the shatterproof glass. One by one we were sent to the attic to see a middle-aged woman with a nervous laugh, somebody they called 'the employment consultant'. The real purpose of the course was to get us off benefits, and fast. I was sitting on the pavement outside, trying to stretch a cigarette break to an hour, quickly thinking up cheap methods of avoiding the agency's attempt to employ me. Marcus Lawry was on his way back from the news section in Smith's where he'd read the guitar magazines from cover to cover. That afternoon we paired up for a communication exercise. We talked about bands when we'd finished with time to spare.

Rock music was on a downer. The Seattle guitar bands disintegrated when Kurt Cobain killed himself at the top of his game. He fell out of our lives, unfinished. The media attention and the endless rounds of Nirvana's MTV Unplugged only emphasised his absence. Had he lived, kids would have grown bored of his alienation-incited movement and begun their own contrary music scene. As it was, they had to start from scratch. Seven years had passed and nothing as life-affirming as grunge had shot up to replace it. The mainstream was even less hopeful. The media-induced phenomenon of Brit Pop, and the Blur v Oasis showdown, collapsed when Tony Blair got his guitar out of its dusty case. The Cool Cymru phenomenon riding on its back did nothing more than highlight the mediocrity of the Stereophonics and the now Richey-less Manic Street Preachers. An appalling faux talent show called *Pop Idol* was being aired on primetime television in which ordinary people competed for record contracts simply by standing up and singing old Kylie Minogue songs. It brought a culture of immediate stardom completely lacking in merit and creativity. But it was popular and therefore lucrative. Major record companies seemed unwilling suddenly to draw up double album deals. If a debut failed to chart, its architect had little prospect. Individuality got lost somewhere between the end of Thatcher's era and the beginning of Blair's. Teenagers, regardless of their tastes, all looked the same, hanging around supermarket car parks in their uniform black hooded sweatshirts. The Noughties still had a hangover from the Nineties and music was struggling into the new decade.

After a reasonably active period, the music scene in the Rhondda had been reduced to a bank holiday gig at a Workingmen's Club. In 1976, local blues band The Racing Cars hit the top ten of the charts with 'They Shoot Horses, Don't They?' But the emergence of punk split them up soon after, and they became backing musicians for various other acts, including Tina Turner. Now they were back in their original guise filling dance floors before and after the bingo. Original music, for the moment at least, had perished.

My new friend who managed a local punk band, reckoned that just below the surface were hundreds of young guitar bands playing an indefinable blend of pop, punk, electronica and grunge, all of the last decade's influences combined; the bastard children of indifference. Of course they had nowhere to play and nowhere to be seen and therefore remained unsigned. The Lostprophets, a band from 'here', Marcus said, pointing adamantly at the threadbare carpet of the classroom, had gone to LA to escape this obscure fate, and would later emerge as a transatlantic 'nu-metal' phenomenon. Another fanzine coined description was *emo*, short for 'emotional hardcore', the music typified by stop and start guitars. It was business as usual apparently, and if Marcus could only make it through the course without getting a job, he'd study music promotion at college and restart a Rhondda band night.

On a Wednesday afternoon the agency sent us on an

31

orienteering programme at Taff Vale Farm, a miniature version of the team building weekends where international banks send their senior staff. It involved looking for envelopes hidden in the foliage with the aid of a compass, balancing on mossy tree trunks propped over sheep dips, walking backwards through fast flowing streams. The finale was a mile-long rat-infested tunnel buried deep into the mountain. The idea of the mission was to split us into groups and send us in at either mouth – we'd pass one another somewhere along the intestine and the first group out intact won the challenge. We filed into the darkness on our knees. Soon the shaft of sunlight beaming in behind us disappeared and the heat became restrictive, the stagnant water underneath us sloshing about. The tar keeping the corrugated zinc roof together was melting under the summer heat, dripping onto the backs of our T-shirts. Everyone was suffocating. We passed the other group at what seemed like ten minutes in, limbs touching limbs, shoulders shouldering shoulders. In the blackness all sense of time and distance dissolved. The only other girl on the course was leading; a petite eighteen-year-old with blonde hair and pink, glittery trainers. She halted regularly, thinking she'd touched the wet fur of a rat. 'I can see them,' she screeched, 'their eyes are fuckin' shining.' The boy at the back pushed ahead, rushing her. We all piled into one another, foreheads touching arse-cheeks. Marcus was behind me and kept butting my undercarriage so I was forced to jump away from him and butt the boy in front. Every time the girl paused, terrified, the boy came back, forcing my arse into Marcus' face. The scuttling conveyor-belt of forced closeness carried on up 'til the exit. We won the challenge with an easy seven-minute lead on the other team.

On the way back to the farmhouse the steroid-fattened trainer found a wide tree stump in the middle of the field. He split us up again. He was going to buy a pub lunch for the team who could get all their feet touching the stump. The other group went first, five of them managing to stand on the surface while the others stood around it, staring at it vacantly. On our turn Marcus ordered us all to the floor and we pushed our sopping trainers up against the bark, lying back like rays shooting out of a sun. If the ability to earn money really was linked to skill and determination, neither Marcus nor me would have been there prostituting ourselves for a giro on a flaming hot afternoon. But why should we work in factories when we could manage bands and write bestsellers? We thought our ambition gave us the right to use the benefit system to our own ends. Our problem was that we'd given ourselves permission to aspire. By the beginning of 2002 my novel had won an Orange Futures Prize. Marcus had set a record label up from his bedroom. Poisoned Whiskey Records put shows on at the local Workingmen's and saved the entry fee to pay for studio time for the local bands. Eventually he'd release their mini-albums and EPs. He had a regular Friday night show at the Rhondda Hotel, a pub at the top of Cymmer hill. Bands played on the stage in the first floor function room and Marcus stood on the steep landing, ink-stamping wrists. Most of it melded into a forgettable blur of reverb; the music a badly mixed cocktail of grunge and punk, both elements watered down to vacuity.

It was at the Rhondda Hotel that I first encountered a four-piece called Midasuno. I noticed the frontman first. He had hair like Trent Reznor. I watched him as he got onstage with his band mates; valley kids in scruffy jeans, and the buzz of conversation quietened down. They looked like a gaggle of mental patients with a literally larger than life drummer beating his skins to tears. The guitarists thrashed their instruments around unpredictably, the frontman's mascara ran in sweaty rivulets down his face. They played a song called 'Cut Ribbons', a compound of alternative, indie, hardcore, metal and punk, urgent, industrial and somehow, sometimes melodic. The chorus seemed only to consist of these words: 'She came home, broke my bones, then she cut ribbons out of me. She came home; broke my bones, then she cut ribbons out of me. She came home; broke my bones, then she cut ribbons out of me.' I'm not sure if it was this, the hazy subject matter, which impressed me (I'd grown up after all with the fairly misogynistic attitudes of traditional rock stars who wrote about the ease with which they frequently took whores, not got beaten up by them) or the utter passion with which it was delivered. The bizarre spectacle ended with the frontman screaming, 'CHA CHA CHA, BOOM, YEAH! CHA CHA CHA, BOOM, YEAH!' while the bass drum shook the room. Extreme, no frills, balls out rock. It was the most compelling thing I'd ever seen in what was a space designed for engagement parties. Where the other bands seemed to be forcing round pegs in square holes, here everything fit and the X Factor which record executives talk so fervently about this band had in abundance.

On a Sunday morning, two days later, I awoke to the sound of my fiancé Darran, screeching vociferously over a frying pan of bacon. We'd met a week into the Millennium, fallen in love in a fortnight, and moved in together within a month. Now he was part of me – as indispensable as a vital organ. 'BOOM, CHAKA, YEAH,' he was shouting. 'BOOM CHAKA BOOM, BOOM.' He flipped the meat in the pan over so the oil sizzled in time with his rendition. 'Can't get this stupid boom thing out of my mind,' he said when I'd got downstairs.

'You know what it is, don't you?' I said.

He shook his head.

'It's that band from Merthyr. It's one of their songs.'

Later that day we drove to the Tesco Superstore outside Pontypridd. As we walked across the car-park we saw the band we'd been talking about leave, swaggering along the forecourt in T-shirts and dirty denim, the frontman's black hair riotous. Juxtaposed against the calm afternoon, they looked like squally pirates clutching their loot to their chests, about to make off to the next town they'd terrorize. Even buying brunch they *looked* like a rock band.

'It's that band,' Darran said, pointing.

I nodded. With hindsight it's easy to see it as a prophetic moment, foretelling me of the way Midasuno would thump in and out of my life.

The Red Mist

It was the beginning of a brand new century. Matt yanked the door of his parents' garage open and walked towards his drum kit. It was colder inside than out; the coloured cardboard of the egg boxes fading and falling from the walls, their adhesive dried to nothing. He sat down and mindlessly beat the skin of the snare, waiting for the others to turn up with their unreliable equipment. Gavin Jessop was playing bass, Steven Hopkins, guitar. Scott had long since assumed the role of enigmatic frontman. They were all seventeen, a year out of school and marginally employed in the local retail and service industries. 1999 had been a big Welsh year. The National Assembly had opened in Cardiff, giving the country its first political command centre. European Union funding filtered slowly into the Valleys, enticing new business to the area. Out of town retail parks grew out of the wastelands surrounding Merthyr; fast food restaurants, DIY superstores, Brewer's Fayre pubs. For the first time since the iron boom, work was plentiful in Merthyr and far from the perilous physical labour of the collieries and ironworks it was risk-free, anodyne employment, flipping burgers and operating tills – more likely to bore you to death than contaminate or maim. Even Welsh music was attracting national press attention. Although it was pop music, insipid for the most part, it stamped our nationality on the charts. Super Furry Animals and Catatonia were massive. Aberdare band the Stereophonics had released their second album after three years in the limelight.

Rumour had it that when Richard Branson rang frontman Kelly Jones' house offering 'the deal', his mother had disbelievingly answered, 'Yeah, right, and I'm Elizabeth Taylor.' Matt didn't particularly like any of the music engaged in the Cool Cymru episode because it wasn't metal, it was pop. He only hoped there'd be curiosity enough left to accommodate his own band.

Scott had written two songs, namely 'Tear', an anthemic guitar and drum gala about some weird fantasy he had of getting kidnapped by a zealous and angry woman, and 'The Art of Fear', an acerbic, Gothic spine-chiller aimed at the bigoted and sceptical populace of their hometown. What they lacked in original material they'd made up for with well chosen covers. At their first gig in their new guise as a four-piece they'd played for fifteen minutes to a zombie-like crowd at Treharris Boys' Club before attempting a Stereophonics song. The crowd suddenly erupted, braying for an encore. Surreptitiously they returned to their own stuff, slowly but surely influencing the audience. Their new name was Midasuno, a rushed amalgamation of a character in Matt's favourite video-game and Scott's favourite Muse song. This was their assembly, set to send them kicking into the new Millennium.

Midasuno's first gigs were aggressive. Scott, in an attempt to stage a visually arresting performance, would swing his guitar around by its neck, sometimes hitting another band member. It was nothing new. We'd all seen bands let rip on their equipment; smash an electric guitar to wooden pieces, throw a drum at an amplifier stack. Everyone expected this kind of destruction, even if the guitar Scott was lamping around happened to be his only one. What was unusual is that the other band members would quite often respond, hitting him with their own instruments. Scott would pick his guitar up by its headstock with his mouth and Matt would throw a drum at him. Steven, feeling snubbed, would deliberately knock his guitar head against Scott's face. Scott, shaking with adrenaline, would find an empty chair in the auditorium and whack it across the back of somebody's head. They were what Scott calls his 'red-mist moments', the discharge of unknown quantities of pure rage. They set a precedent, turning live shows into a blast of blood-soaked stirring rock music offset by impromptu wrestling matches. Maybe it was this unpredictability which impressed industry magazine *Sound Nation* journalist James McLaren in early 2002 and Jo Hunt from Community Music Wales. Hunt arranged them as support to the prodigal return of the Lostprophets in a series of showcases at the Blackwood Miners Institute. A few months later, when McLaren set up his own Cardiff-based independent record label and called it Cascade, he asked the band if they'd care to be his first release. 'The Art of Fear' was recorded at Frontline Studios in Caerphilly, produced by Lostprophets bassist, Stuart Richardson.

In the November of that year, Midasuno were summoned to the annual Welsh Music Awards ceremony, nominated as Best New Unsigned Band. There were three other bands in the same category including The Kennedy Soundtrack and hotly tipped neophytes, Funeral for a Friend. Few people expected the band to triumph over the much-hyped competition, least of all Midasuno. Nevertheless, it was an invitation to a party, their absolute favourite pastime, and they dressed for it in ties and trouser suits. Their table was loaded with alcohol: the usual beer and champagne, as well as countless wines that Gavin had never encountered before. He quickly set to work on the Jagermeister. In the lavatory he'd stood between Stuart and Jamie from the Lostprophets, slandering the guitarist of The Kennedy Soundtrack while they urinated. Back in the auditorium, the guitarist of The Kennedy Soundtrack walked by the Midasuno table. Gavin smiled and waved. When actor Gary Beadle, (known to the band only as Paul Truman from *EastEnders*) announced the award, Matt was blind drunk. A girl sitting next to him shook him and told him he'd won. Scott and Gavin and Steven were on the stage in an eighth of a second. Matt followed, glancing uncertainly around the auditorium. From the podium Gavin could see Scott's girlfriend trampolining on her chair, hunks of its stuffing grasped in her balled-up fists. The no swearing policy the band had been warned about a month previously was blatantly and immediately disregarded. The first word out of Scott's mouth was 'fuck.' 'Fuck. Thank you. Fuck. We'd just like to, er, fucking thank every fucker who voted for us or whatever. Fucking hell. Thanks. Fuck.' The award, a silver, triangular structure, was planted firmly in his armpit as he pulled away from the microphone to tell the presenter that he watched him in *EastEnders*, and wrote all of his best stuff when it was on. When they were leaving the ceremony that evening, tremendously intoxicated and highly emotional, a fight somehow broke out between Scott and Matt. They were standing on the red carpet at the entrance to the Coal Exchange, sparring pathetically, when Matt's trousers fell down. Rather than disrupt the skirmish to pick them up, he grabbed Scott by one of his lapels and managed to get a fist in. Some of the paparazzi waiting impatiently in the cold for the Lostprophets and Amy Wadge to emerge took a couple of photographs. Greg Haver, producer of Manic Street Preachers B-sides and producer of Midasuno's only B-side, stepped in to disturb the increasingly belligerent spat. Instantly, Scott and Matt ceased to beat one another and both turned on the interloper.

When the awards were televised a few weeks later, the Unsigned Band Award was announced by a voice-over, a still photograph of the band positioned in the centre of the black screen. Their reputation as a hard drinking, hard fighting, party band was cemented.

Dial M for Merthyr

Pontypridd Railway Station has the longest platform in Europe. I know it like the back of my hand; a Victorian structure where miners from the three adjoining valleys congregated at the height of the industrial age for union meetings and rugby matches, the mile-long strings of cars, filled with coal, pummelled over the tracks. In the summer between my first and second years of university I worked the afternoon shift in an electronics factory on Treforest Industrial Estate – making an LED display for the Chilean government. There was an hour between the end of my shift and the last train home where I'd stand alone in the dark, imagining the station's history. It was years later now, early on a Friday morning in April 2003. As I alighted from the train carriage, the flaps and squawks of pigeons quarrelling over the breakfast pastry echoed under the fibre glass shelters. Scott was standing beneath the eaves, the same long, black, dishevelled hair, big, dark circles under his eyes, peering at me inquisitively as I approached him, blood-red nail polish daubed on his fingers.

'How are you?' he asked, pleasantly.

I replied positively, lying. My legs were numb with apprehension. I was starting to feel sick. Two months earlier, a new English band called The Darkness had played at the Pop Factory. My brother-in-law urged me to buy tickets. They were my kind of music, he said, he'd seen them before. I agreed, not because I trusted his judgement but because Midasuno were the support act. We were sitting in a pub a few yards away from the venue waiting for my brother-in-law and his girlfriend; it was empty save for a few kids playing pool and the barflies huddling around the pumps. Something that must be understood about the Rhondda is that quite a lot of its inhabitants are alcoholics. Many simply live in the lounges of pubs – they have their giros sent to the landlords and in return the landlord provides breakfast and all the cider slops they can drink. The Llwyncelyn's is a deaf man called Benny. We were two or three sips into our appetisers when he undid his fly and pissed against the bar.

We were late arriving at the Pop Factory. Midasuno were packing up. The Darkness came out of their dressing room and set up. The frontman performed the first song in pink leather trousers, sweaty from swinging around on the rafters. Later, two female members of his entourage jumped on stage to undress him, revealing his zebra-print cat-suit. He folded the cat-suit down to his waist where a tattooed roll of flame licked up out of his crotch, kitsch gimmicks: obviously. They were supposed to be a joke band, a latter day Spinal Tap, but I missed the punch-line because they played the most irresistible AC/DC-inspired guitar riffs. There was an overwhelming sense

44

of euphoria in every falsetto lyric he forced out of his throat and that is what rock music at its boldest was meant to sound like. Impatient with the grey, characterless, soulless soundtrack the Noughties had provided, I was immediately hooked. I couldn't help thinking that a fragment of rock history was being formed right there in my presence. After the show the frontman came around to meet everyone. I shook his hand, staring at the perspiration-damp tendrils of hair clinging to his balding forehead, knowing even as I did that I was going to let this man who had amazed me walk away without a word of acclaim. A lot of people think I'm arrogant but actually I'm just shy.

'I told you,' my brother-in-law said. 'Didn't I tell you?'

Well, what did he expect? I'd fed and watered myself on cock rock since the tender age of twelve. I used to stuff the bandana my mother tied over her rollers into my denim arse pocket because it was similar, slightly, to the one Steven Tyler tied to his microphone stand. For the first time, in a very long time, joke or not – I felt like part of something.

Almost unconsciously, the narrator of my novel in progress had become a music journalist. (It was the only way I could get her within fucking distance of Kelly Jones and was what I myself had always wanted to be.) The world was in the centre of a new rock-writing renaissance so I rang The Darkness' press agent and asked her for an interview. They were too busy.

We walked very quickly across the intersection, the little man in the pedestrian signal flashing green. Scott was chatting incessantly. I wasn't listening to him; it was too much to take in. This was my first bona fide music interview and I could hear the thrum of my blood pulsing anxiously, breath-like in my ear canals. Market Street coiled towards the town centre, the tips of the buildings obscured by fog. Angharad's was closed. I pointed at the Café Royale, a pre-war tea-house where valley people went to chain-smoke. Scott paused mid-sentence and nodded. When I asked him what he wanted, he said, 'Anything that's really cheap.' He'd missed a music production lecture at the university to come and talk to me. The other band members were at work. He'd tried to work at McDonalds for two months but didn't trust himself around the till. 'I told them I'd steal the money,' he said, his eyes widening. 'It's simple. You only work for money so if the money's right there in front of you, you're going to pick it up and run.' I needn't have worried about my as yet non-existent interviewing technique. Scott was a media whore, both candid and charming with a magnificent gift for guessing what you wanted to hear and telling it to you quickly, like a sweet information stab to the jugular; articulate and utterly quotable. As he spoke he reached over his shoulder to touch a new wound that habitually reopened; the result of his frantic showmanship. He had damaged much of the equipment, injured all of the other band members and to date, five or six fans.

'I'm in and out of hospital all the time,' he said, blowing his hair out of his face. He gave me a run down of Midasuno's activities over the past three years.

In 2001 when they'd started playing gigs outside their own neighbourhood, Scott attracted a stalker. It was a woman who made abusive and threatening phone-calls to his parental home; Dial M for Merthyr. She'd tell him to break the band up or else she'd do it for him. Scott realised he'd touched a nerve. Jealousy had reared its head; a typical working-class plague, rife in the South Wales Valleys. In response he'd written the caustic lyrics to 'The Art of Fear'.

Shortly afterwards they supported the Wildhearts at the Coal Exchange. The Wildhearts are one of both mine and Scott's favourite bands. Before the Midasuno supported gig, I'd last seen them live at St David's Hall in 1993. I was fourteen years old. At the end of the show, the frontman, Ginger, came out into the foyer to sign tickets. My school friend who was with me had been drinking cider all day and didn't believe that it actually was Ginger. Like my mother, she had an annoying habit of talking in a ridiculous English accent as soon as the alcohol hit the bloodstream. She walked straight up to him and said, 'You're not Ginger. Stop defacing all these poor people's souvenirs.' The words came out in a West Country hybrid which even Ginger deduced as fake. He repeated her sentence, now also assuming this bizarre pronunciation, which on top of his broad Geordie accent sounded even more hilarious. He looked at me and we both bent over laughing.

'Sorry,' I said, apologising for my friend.

He cupped my face in his hands. 'S'orright, pet,' he said.

At the Wildhearts gig in 2002, Ginger stood stage-side to watch the whole of the support band's set. 'It wasn't that long ago I was saving coppers and taking them to the record fairs at Cyfarthfa to see which Japanese Wildhearts import I could afford next,' Scott said.

Now he was a boy on the precipice between nobody and celebrity, his band the best kept secret in Wales. I imagined the valleys like a three-legged squid, the head as Pontypridd and the orbs on the end of the tentacles as the Rhondda, Aberdare and Merthyr. Inside the orbs were villages, each one mirroring one another. Dissatisfaction had made him pick up a guitar like I'd picked up a biro. We were two versions of the same brain, both discontented by pussy music with no clitoris.

The cappuccino was cold and untouched, the questions on my jotter pad long exhausted. He gave me a scratched up promo CD. I gave him a copy of my novel, which he took on tour. We left each other at the traffic lights. When I got home I wrote the story. Three days later I sold it.

When Bulls Play God

Glamorgan University was about to break up for the Easter holiday. It was 2003, daffodils springing yellow from the borders of the knolls. Scott was walking away from a Thursday morning lecture in the vast glass tower of G Block, towards a lunchtime seminar in an annexe at the entrance of the University site, the arts department and oldest division of the building, looking out over Treforest Industrial Estate where a trail of electronic factories and cash and carries dominoed down either side of the river. Students dawdled along the pathways. He was studying music technology, and nearing the end of his first year. His attempts at formal employment radically unsuccessful, study was a constructive method of killing time while he waited for Midasuno's eventual glory. Local press interest was intense; he juggled interviews with lectures, band rehearsal with study, and a growing itinerary of gigs with his increasing amount of coursework. He was

49

approaching the B Block vestibule with its paved courtyard and tin ashtrays, yards away from Tom Jones' former local, the Otley Arms, when his phone rang. A representative from Worcester-based company, Lockjaw Records, told him that they'd like to sign the band. They'd seen them playing recently at a venue in Worcester and would like to fund their first album. A meeting at Merthyr Wetherspoons was arranged for the following week. Scott put his telephone back in his coat pocket. This is it, he thought. The band met with the Lockjaw A&R on a Wednesday evening, the contract set down on the table between them. The pub was empty save for the bar staff grudgingly polishing the furniture.

'Take your time,' the representative said, ordering another round. 'Think it through.' The band reached for the biro as soon as the door had flapped closed behind him.

That summer Midasuno set up camp in an anonymous north Wales cottage to record their debut mini-album. Portmeirion, best known as 'The Village' in the 1960s British cult TV series *The Prisoner*, housed The Waiting Room recording studio where they'd work and live for a tight five-day schedule, complying to the two thousand pound budget. The theatrical location, including a neoclassical colonnade, Siamese figures on ionic columns, a Jacobean town hall, a Buddha and Italianate campanile, was to all intents and purposes a private village, closed in the evening to the public. With Porthmadog, the nearest town, an hour's walk away, Lockjaw was stringent in its measures to keep the band sober and dutiful. What it didn't bank on were water pistols. The members took one each and in the absence of pubs to patronize and girls, or indeed any other human beings, to meet, they christened their temporary home with a Goliath war game, dousing the luxurious chaise longue in the process. Album producers Ray Tibbets and Nigel Shipley arrived in the midst of the battle, the realisation of their assignment suddenly dawning on them. One week later however, the house guests emerged with a six song EP. They called it *When Bulls Play God*, the name a result of a drinking session in front of the student house portable TV. A 'when animals attack' style programme aired footage of a bull tearing a Spanish picador to strips, and the words fell from Scott's mouth; Scott instantly aware of their ambiguity. The album was released in the autumn, its case a red background decorated with simple black bull-shaped silhouettes and toy ticker-tape text, designed by school acquaintance and fellow music technology student, Lyndon Jones.

In less than three years, the band had established a direction, a reputation, signed a record contract and released their debut album. In the time-honoured tradition they were sent by their record company to endorse themselves on a national scale. Albums didn't sell themselves. It was time for Midasuno's first live tour. At the average age of twenty, the band had never left Troedyrhiw for more than a fortnight; valley bumpkins setting out on the rock circuit journey of their lives. The idea of it smacked of Guns 'n' Roses *Welcome to the Jungle* video, where Axl Rose stepped down from a Greyhound bus and into Los Angeles, a chewed stalk of straw still held between his gritted teeth.

Matt's father, John Riste, recently injured in a work accident, was now permanently at the band's disposal. He offered to drive the tour bus, a covert mode of insuring the band didn't enter harm's way, and he agreed to adopt the foreign moniker of 'tour manager' and subsist in the tour bus cab, divorced by a curtain from the kids who'd been rehearsing

51

in his garage for twelve years. The van hit the road in November 2003, visiting Southampton, Cornwall, Hull, Liverpool, Nottingham and London. Subject for the first time to riders (products with which the venue or gig promoter, as part payment, try to appease the band during the run up to their performance and usually consisting of alcohol) Midasuno quickly equated touring to an almost never-ending party. It contained all of the vital ingredients: themselves, booze, music and hordes of decidedly grateful girls. What was more, it was a soiree on the move, jumping from one setting to the next, the guests' accents perpetually varying, and the girls incessantly eager. The days were erratic and novel. They ended adrenaline-soaked and exultant, in anonymous lay-bys on nameless stretches of motorways, the band throwing bottles at one another whilst trying to relieve themselves in pitch-black fields.

They began again with hangovers, curable only with more alcohol. Gavin took snap shot memories home, vague and interchangeable images; blowing the headline band off the stage, going punch for punch with Matt in the tour bus gangway until he was too exhausted to even lift his arms, washing Scott's naked back down with the lemons from the rider during a shared post-gig shower. The band as a whole would never really be the same again. Now they'd discovered a blissful means of temporarily escaping Merthyr; a delirious working holiday, free of rule and convention.

A Detour

A fortnight after my interview with Scott, The Darkness were back at the Pop Factory filming a performance for a television show. It was my second chance to tell frontman Justin Hawkins what I thought of him; just one magic sentence that would make him notice me above all the other women he had ever met, as the one who'd empathise with his art. The doors opened at six. It was 2.30 in the afternoon. My sister-in-law drove me to her house where we spent the remainder of the day drinking Lambrini, her favourite wine, and quite possibly the cheapest alcoholic drink on the market (7.5% and £2 per 150cl).

Very often I think I'm the only person in the world who understands how it feels to love a band *so* much, it starts to hurt. I'm completely obsessive of course, but there's a vital motive for people to become aficionados of music and football and whatever it is that captures their imagination. A long time ago we had legends and folklore. Characters like Robin Hood,

Owain Glyndwr and Boudicca were knocking around; warriors who had superhuman strength, wisdom, courage and agility. Romantic anecdotes grew around them like gardens because of communication gaps in generations; Chinese whispers. And they just kept getting stronger. Now we expect nothing less than perfection, we want to see people of our own lifetime with the same sort of potency, because their passion, their clout – it's the same stuff us mortals have in us, but in us, it's dormant. We don't have the determination it requires to rebuff junk-food and sex in order to play football on a Saturday. We don't have the tenacity to struggle through the penniless years of grafting for a record contract so we let our idols do it for us. It isn't worship; it's a lazy form of revelation. Deep, deep down, we *understand*: they're our spokespeople. Rock stars fill up an emotional hole in my brain which is desperate for a hero, and because I'm a girl and quite often they are boys, I tend to think that sleeping together could help us share our mettle.

The Darkness had signed a major record deal the previous day. They were in a celebratory mood. For two years they'd been virtually ignored by record companies who thought they couldn't market such a flamboyant act. The band had self financed their album with Justin's sideline (he wrote jingles for IKEA). Now they were attracting a blaze of publicity and Warner wanted in. During their performance, two things worthy of note happened. Firstly, the white Lycra cat-suit that Justin was wearing burst at the hem of his inside thigh. Amidst a handstand, his right testicle fell out. He laid helplessly on the stage while the floor manager procured a roll of electrical tape and awkwardly glued him up. It was nice. It introduced a measure of vulnerability into the equation. Secondly, Justin winked at me. The song he was singing at the time was called

'Growing on Me': 'I can't get rid of you, I don't know what to do, I don't even know who is growing on who.' In my drunken reverie I began to believe that Justin, despite himself, was getting a crush on me. I worked out much later that the song was an ode to genital warts. After the show he came out of his dressing room, walking towards me. The magnificent, life-changing speech I had written in my head had been lost to hours of incoming wine. 'Did women fancy you when you were fat?' I said, because I'd read in an interview somewhere that he'd lost weight to squeeze into those leotards. He giggled timidly and retreated back into his dressing room.

By October, my fixation with the band had gradually transformed itself into ambition. I had a demented notion that if I wrote a book about them, a kind of warts 'n' all tour diary which required my constant presence on their bus, I could make Justin fall in love with me (like he had with his manager, Sue, his common law wife). *The Big Issue* sent me to the Pop Factory to report on the annual music award ceremony and The Darkness were due to sweep the board. Justin didn't turn up, supposedly suffering with an ailing throat. At the after-show party I found Frankie Poullain, the bassist, loafing around the free bar, a vodka tumbler fixed to his moustached mouth. I put my lip-gloss on and approached him.

'You're half-French,' I said, passing him a cigarette. I rose up like a ballerina on the toes of my slouch-boots (the Pop Factory floor, a checkerboard of raised terracotta tiles that once drained carbonated liquid spills away, discouraged silly fuck-me shoes). I pouted and fluttered my lashes. 'I'm half-Italian.'

Frankie smiled. His great grandfather was a writer, he said, and he'd always had a particular fondness for writers, and me writing a book about the band sounded like a bloody good idea.

By the end of the night I was in the foyer with him and the drummer and a horde of very thin, blonde Scandinavian women who had starred in their latest video. Their limousine was waiting. 'Are you coming?' Frankie asked, filching his room key out of his coat and showing me the Celtic Manor emblem embossed on the ring. Coyly, I shook my head and wrote the name of my novel on two separate pieces of paper, stuffing them into the band members' pockets. I wasn't sure how famous you had to be before maids started laundering your trousers. Perhaps they'd actually find them. I rang the management office three hundred times between then and December but Sue never accepted my call. I decided that she was jealous of me. A quickly-produced tabloidesque biography hit the bookshelves in time for Christmas.

There were two other rock bands at the after-show party that night and when my infatuation with Justin had worn away but my drive to work on a documentary hadn't, I split my hunger between them. In America the Lostprophets had hit superstar status. Snubbed by their insistence on staying in the US, the British music press had begun to condemn them as an alternative boy band, cruising through on their looks alone, and there were rumours that their LA stylists had made them get tattoos so they looked less like Mammy's boy A Level students. This changed when they released 'Burn, Burn', the first single from their new album. Their sound had been polished to perfection, their singer could suddenly sing and it charted at no.17. They were famous now and to prove it one of them started going out with a *Top of the Pops* presenter.

I was convinced that they were the band I should focus on, partly because I wanted to explore their Catherine Zeta Jones-style rise to notoriety but also because I'd chatted briefly to the keyboard player at the party. He'd told me he'd gone to watch Pontypridd play rugby at Sardis Road the night before, only to discover that Pontypridd were now the Celtic Warriors – a regional side paired with Bridgend. At the end of his rant he took his cowboy boot off to show me the socks he'd bought on tour in Japan; grey woollies with sleeves for each of his gnarly toes. The band had left for America again but the keyboard player, who was also an artist, had left some of his paintings at a local exhibition in a nearby hotel. I visited the curator and told him that I'd buy his centre-piece for double its price if he would give me the artist's personal telephone number. He refused. With retrospect it's fortunate he did. I didn't have the money to buy it at its original mark-up. Then, later on in the year I was sitting in a Cardiff Burger King when I saw one of the guitarists from the band pass the window. I left my cheeseburger and followed him into an arcade where he was buying shoes for his girlfriend. I told him I wanted to write something about the band and he wrote his agent's e-mail address in my notebook. It felt like destiny. After two months without a reply I realised it was a red herring.

At the beginning of the decade, Funeral for a Friend were just one of the many emo acts playing locally and putting EPs out on small Welsh labels, but after the transatlantic success of the Lostprophets eyes turned to South Wales in search of the next triumph. The eyes chose Funeral, notwithstanding their problematic name which is apparently a song by a Florida band called Planes Mistaken for Stars, but also one by Elton John on the *Yellow Brick Road* album. *Kerrang!* in a shock announcement, labelled them the best band on the planet. Their debut, *Casually Dressed and Deep in Conversation*, spawned three hit songs, one of which was 'Juneau'. It had the tag-lyric, 'I'm nothing more than a line in your book', which I took to be an omen. I met Darran, one of the guitarists, at the following year's Pop Factory Awards and asked him if he'd consider a documentary. 'A book?' he said. 'Nah, that's a naff thing to do. That's something The Darkness would do.' I smiled through gritted teeth. 'And anyway,' he said, 'our singer's uncle fancies himself as a writer. If we were going to say yes we'd let him do it.' He turned to my fiancé and began a conversation about the merits of being called Darran spelt with an A.

I realised in that split second that my lust for rock music, with all of its gloss and sparkle, had got in the way of my integrity. For two whole years I'd been hanging around like a star-fucker; my ability to see beyond drivel clouded by champagne – a girl who almost became a body part in a orgy on the marble floor of a hotel bathroom while Darran waited patiently for me at home. In 2002, only two years before, Midasuno had beaten Funeral for a Friend to the Welsh Music Awards Best Unsigned Band label. The after show parties had been a luxurious decoy keeping me from looking at what was plain in front of my face – if I was going to write a book about a rock band, I might as well write about a real one. Midasuno had character, passion and guts. What's more, I was sure that they would be willing to bare all.

Out to Lunch

The pub lounge smelt of furniture polish and fabric freshener. It wasn't eleven o'clock yet, the barmaid wasn't serving alcohol. We ordered Coca Cola to pass the time. While she poured it Scott made a prophetic stab at conversation; 'It's a bummer that Hunter S Thompson died, ain't it?' I looked at him incredulously. Unless he was a clairvoyant of the highest standard possible, he didn't know that the notebook in my handbag was littered with references to Thompson which I was about to use to try to entice him into letting me on the band's official tour bus. 'Yes, it is,' I said, dazedly. I had only found out he'd shot himself the previous night whilst listening by chance to the Radio 2 News.

'Cheers mate,' the barmaid said as she put the soda down in front of me, as though she recognised I was a woman of the world who could do pretty much anything a bloke could, which seemed to forebode well for a summer on the road, drinking

Cobra with the boys, carrying amplifiers in and out of venues.

Since we'd last met, Midasuno's situation had thoroughly altered. Their relationship with Lockjaw had gone badly and the contract had been revoked. Now the band were as unsigned and insolvent as they had been on the day they were created. To complicate matters further, guitarist Steven Hopkins had suddenly quit. It was September 2004, a week before the band was due to start a tour, when he rang Scott announcing his abrupt departure. He didn't enjoy touring anymore; he wanted to concentrate on his degree. That left Matt Riste, Gavin Jessop and Scott. Bereft of rehearsal time, they attempted an imminent warm-up show as a three-piece; a catastrophe which discouraged them even entertaining the idea of ever playing as a trio again. They were on their way home from that gig, the tour bus lounge numb with the lacklustre post-gig atmosphere, when they realised they'd need to audition a new guitarist; a stranger, a gatecrasher. Scott could pinpoint the exact scene. They were driving out of Cardiff, towards the Valleys, along a street famed locally for the house with the Christmas trimmings. (Anytime between October and New Year you can marvel at the preposterous sum of tasteless decorations strung around the property; illuminated reindeer and singing Santas – every year it makes the Welsh news.) Gavin was ripping his favourite pictures out of a pornographic magazine, licking them so they'd stick to the tour bus window; indolent and half cut. 'We're going to have to get a guitarist,' Scott said, sighing. Matt concurred.

During his second year at university, one of Scott's music technology assignments had been to produce a recording. Whilst looking for a band about to make a demo, he encountered a local punk outfit, The UCA Chapter. They'd played at RM's, Merthyr's primary rock club, and played a radiant cover of an AFI song. Scott shaped their demo, becoming friends with guitarist Chris Morgan in the process. Chris was a zealous seventeen-year-old, obsessed with the pre-Richey-disappearance Manic Street Preachers and New York punk icons, The Ramones. He was three years old when *Appetite for Destruction* was released and had grown up surrounded by rugby fans in the town of Tredegar in the Rhymney Valley, harassed on a daily basis for his band T-shirts and dyed black hair. Chris took to alternative rock like a pin to a magnet. He started his first band at the age of eleven and had continued regardless ever since; becoming more dogged every time one of the dance kids struck him with a two pence coin or a rugby player punched him in the street. Matt rang Chris and asked him to come to band practice. Five seconds into 'Tear', Scott knew it was going to work. Chris joined the band on tour the following week. He fell seamlessly into the routine, and was unconcerned by the spectacle of Gavin trying to wind his penis around the tour bus gear stick. Lyndon Jones, designer of the band artwork and website, had also joined as a keyboardist, sampler and sound effects layer. They were all currently recording Midasuno's self-financed second album, which they intended to call *Songs in the Key of Fuck*, at the Strongbox Studios in Penarth. Scott, Gavin and Lyndon had graduated and were working part-time as shop assistants and waiters, ploughing their wages and spare time into the studio. Chris was sitting his mock A Levels and recording in his revision time as well as attempting to convince his increasingly intolerant teachers that his erratic school attendance was not due to drug addiction or sloth but a progressive and important part of his intended career.

I gave Scott my book proposal, a basic statement about the degree of involvement required, and he shuffled through it with a fixed look of seriousness on his face while I listened with his MP3 player to one of the band's new tracks; a convulsion of drums and guitar with Scott swearing his lungs out above it, like an irate Tasmanian devil. It was incensed and startling, the noise reaching into my head and clinging to the soft sides of my brain matter like an invasive medical instrument. Waitresses were whirling around with the lunchtime orders; hamburgers so perfect they looked like plastic props from *Happy Days*. The pub was filling up with rugby fans. Scott looked up from the proposal for a second and deprecatingly glimpsed around the room. He temporarily forgot the proposition on the table and plunged into a heartfelt monologue, likening Midasuno to a Jurassic Park monster emerging from the sand, en route to trample the hostile and ignorant pockets of mankind; tenacious and hot-blooded as ever. This was customary behaviour. Scott was adept at waxing lyrical in the presence of journalists, but after two years searching for a cooperative band, all I wanted was a yes or a no. Ten minutes into his discourse, I excused myself and went to the toilet. 'You're going to have to sort your bladder problems out,' he said when I got back. 'We only do piss stops every six hundred miles.'

'Are you sure?' I said. (It's my standard response to anyone who is in anyway generous to me. I'm scared that they're going to whip their kindness right back.)

'Yeah,' he said, 'every six hundred miles.'

Part Two

Part Two

The Killing Spoon

It's a Monday night, four days into April. I'm standing at the top of the stainless steel staircase, a green glass bottle of beer in my hand. There are groups of women around me dressed in polka dot and pearls, their long, jet-black hair dreadlocked or backcombed, their chubby feet pushed into Betty Boop platform shoes, eyebrows embellished with kohl, mouths licked with scarlet lipstick, tattooed skin escaping from bustiers, like troupes of burlesque dancers, giggling amongst themselves. The boys wear hooded sweatshirts with white band logos printed on their backs.

This is Clwb Ifor Bach, one of Cardiff's best live venues, tucked neatly into the Womanby Street lanes, only yards away from the Millennium Stadium. This area of the city is its heart. On International days the rugby public eat pre-match breakfasts in greasy spoons. By night, incoming students load up on the Welsh experience. Today, Midasuno kick off their five-day spring tour. We've agreed that I'll join them not for this, but for a leg of their full length summer itinerary. In July their new album should be released. The weather will be kind. This is only a warm-up. But I haven't seen the band play live for over two years. Sometimes, on mention of their name, a member of the local music community says 'Midasuno? Oh, they're the ones with the fat drummer. I thought they'd split up.' I've been dismissing it as petty jealousy but all I know for sure is that they *used* to be good. Cream rises to the top; they may have already curdled.

Dewi, an independent film-maker who has heard about my venture, wants to put a proposal together and pitch it to the BBC – gritty, down-with-the-kids television documentary about a young, valley girl who writes young, gritty novels, writing a gritty, down-with-the-kids documentary about a down-with-the-kids valley band who play gritty rock music: plenty of grit (it's all the rage). He's met me at the club and is drinking a pint of orange squash, re-hydrating his body after a hefty workout. What this exercise is called exactly, he doesn't say, only that it's the same thing the men on the television do between the end of *EastEnders* and the beginning of *Holby City*, which is wear red and white clothing and cartwheel over the roofs of skyscrapers.

Suddenly Scott walks into the bar area and I am the first thing he sees. He's caught for a moment, a deer in my headlights, wondering if he should approach me or turn around and run. He hugs me awkwardly before standing back and lifting his hand to his throat in a gesture which seems to mean his voice is going. He tells us that he's split up with his long-term girlfriend and he's homeless. The pressures of being in the band and of managing it himself have taken a toll on his personal relationships but in the end it was the band which won. He leans in closer to us, staring suspiciously at the crowds around the bar, his eyes sinking back into his skull.

'Know what this band is?' he says conspiratorially, meaning GU Medicine, the one performing before Midasuno. 'They're the band who should be playing at the Titty Twister, the Titty Twister, you know, the club from *Dusk 'Til Dawn*? They sound like somebody trying to kill someone with a spoon.' As he talks he grabs tufts of his black hair and holds them in the air, attacking himself like a trichotillomaniac. 'Imagine it. Imagine trying to kill someone with a spoon.' His tired eyes come alive for a second as he jabs Dewi in the elbow with his finger, an imaginary spoon. 'It'd take ages. Imagine it. It'd take forever to kill someone with a spoon, to actually kill them, gouging and prodding and gouging and fucking prodding.' His speech is working itself up into a crescendo and as I listen I can't help moving closer to him, holding my breath, my teeth fixed together, waiting excitedly for its climax. Dewi's eyes roll anxiously into his head. 'You'd have to tie the spoon to your hand,' Scott says, 'with masking tape. Mask it to your wrist and it'd still take forever, to actually kill someone, ages; forever.'

I've recently heard a rumour about Scott visiting his GP to complain about his insomnia, only to have the doctor tell him that he's delusional. I thought it was a spiteful joke, the delusions in question those of grandeur; Scott believing his success to be bigger than it is. This conversation however, seems to confirm that his mental health may well be on the brink of failure. He is at least presenting himself as a movie-obsessed paranoid schizophrenic. Madness and genius are often flip sides of the same coin. Perhaps I've been looking at

67

the wrong face for half a decade. In any case I'll soon be shacked for a long and sweaty fortnight on a tour bus with him. There'll be time, given that I'm alive and well, to make a comprehensive assessment.

At quarter to eleven, Dewi and I shuffle into the auditorium. We're standing ten rows back and the atmosphere is thick with expectancy. The band are going to play a set of new songs punctuated with only two tracks from their debut. *When Bulls Play God* is done and dusted. They're gearing up for *Songs in the Key of Fuck*. The next time we see Scott he's cradling his guitar, stood behind the microphone in a black suit and skinny tie, globs of green glittery eye-shadow pasted on his eyelids. (Note to self to take care of own make-up.) Chris is a skinny and androgynous teenager; a shop window mannequin dressed up as Johnny Ramone. He delivers the backing vocals, his head jutted towards the microphone; clearly in love with his role. The vibration swells in my throat like a boulder so I'm speechless and unable to turn to Dewi to explain their sound. What I want to tell him, this film-maker who listens to Brazilian drum 'n' bass, is that the Welsh music press have yet to pigeonhole the band because the band insist on disregarding hyphenated sub-genres and will only call themselves 'rock', a term associated with longevity – ensuring fans aren't alienated. Whether that has the opposite effect on record companies we've yet to discover but the fact is they put potential fans before a potential label.

The performance is vicious, the boys jumping around like beans, their guitar heads almost hitting the ceiling, like the forefingers of children trampolining on their parents' mattress. Halfway through a song Scott leaves the microphone to walk over to the bassist and kiss him flatly on the face. When we can't actually see the band for the people in front of us bouncing, we see the base of the microphone stand swing up above them, or a guitar held flat in the air, as though there's some kind of orgy going on just out of view. In Scott's filmic style terms, it's a Welshman who's just got hit in the back by an Englishman's arrow, getting up spitting blood, picking a brick up off the floor and smashing it square in the bowman's jaw. It doesn't take long. It's quick, tight, clean.

'Midasuno rock,' Dewi says, elatedly, as we walk away from the stage, his earlier fears seemingly melted. When we get outside I see the tour van sitting happily on the cobbles like a fat, black pig and I *know* I have a book.

Toilet Circuit Eve

It's the hottest day of the year, thus far. I'm walking up a sharp hill track on the outskirts of Bristol. Towards its summit I can see the stick figures that have gone before me, gathering into a mass like the screen extras of a biblical epic. There's still a long way to go. I suggest we sit down for a moment but my girlfriends, one of whom is actually wearing kitten heels, disagree. If we sit down now, they say, we'll never get up again. The handle of my plastic grocery bag which is stuffed with cans of warm lager chafes my sweating palm. I swap hands and catch them up again, panting. I finally understand why the tickets to Ashton Court only cost £5. You have to put yourself through an ordeal which is the equivalent to rudimentary army training in order to get to the event, and I don't even like the Super Furry Animals – I only came because it was cheap.

It's July 16th, thirteen days exactly since my 27th birthday, when I sat with my friends around my television screen, watching Bob Geldof trying to change the world again, a pitcher of White Russian on the coffee table. My teenage prediction of dying at this very age in a depraved and spectacular Jim Morrison-esque manner now seems increasingly unlikely. I've grown up and begun to appreciate my lot, a detail best illustrated by the comprehensive school kids who hang around our back door, smoking. When we bought the house four years ago, I let them do it – I was probably smoking more in my office at the front of the house. Lately I've been prone to ring the headmistress and report them. Most of my friends are in the puppy stage of their lives; they've bought pedigree dogs on which to practise their parenting skills. Darran's bought a Chelsea Tractor, anticipating five-kid family days out, and in his quest to build a garage to house it has hired a man with a bulldozer who's currently turning my lawn into a 15ft hole. Responsibilities are mounting but my passion for rock music hasn't waned. It's become even more resilient.

I saw Scott by chance recently, when he walked into a Cardiff pub where I was drinking with my poet friend, Clare Potter. It was the Prince of Wales, a Wetherspoons near the station where the great unwashed buy cheap beer after work, or buy cheap beer instead of going to work. A red-eyed Irishman was insisting on telling us his life story, saying he 'grew up too young', a line we'd both try to claim for future pieces, when I noticed Scott standing at the bar with a horde of women dressed in black, his hair highlighted flamingo pink. He came to our table, his head hanging abashed like a naughty kid reporting to its mother. He slipped his sunglasses down his nose and held them cradled in his hand, looking like something transported from Hollywood Boulevard, circa 1987, his eyelids swathed in kohl, a rock star standing on the floral Axminster, surrounded by bemused diners. 'This thing with my girlfriend has been a nightmare,' he said, nodding towards the women, presumably indicating their involvement. He explained that the band was still working on the album and that it might include a cover of the Guns 'n' Roses classic, 'It's So Easy', and that there's a music video in the offing, perhaps directed by Shane Meadows. In a flash of intoxicated intuition I saw how his charm offensive worked. Throwing a mention of Guns 'n' Roses into the conversation was bound to score him points. But how could he possibly know that I'd be familiar with Shane Meadows? That very week I'd been impressed by an illegal copy of *Dead Man's Shoes*, lent to me by my father-in-law.

Since then, Scott's changed his phone number. I've rung him a few times to tell him the BBC have rejected Dewi's proposal, only to reach his T-Mobile answering service. It's a week before the commencement of the Midsummer Murder Tour and I can only hope that he honours his word and takes me with him. The more I contemplate the event, the more foolish it seems to appear. Embarking on a toilet circuit tour of Britain with a bus full of men, average age twenty, is not, as Darran keeps reminding me, a typical or even an acceptable way to spend the summer. I should be eating takeaway and watching romantic comedies on my DVD player with my fiancé and my cat, going to wedding parties and barbeques; wearing pastel-coloured camisoles and sling-backs.

We're close to the entrance and talking about Trent Reznor's muscles, when one of our phones rings. Abi listens to the voice inside the receiver, her mouth falling open, while we stand in a semi circle around her. It's her boyfriend calling from a police station in Prague. All of our boyfriends are in Prague, celebrating a stag weekend together. They've been paintballing this morning only to return to a ransacked apartment. Their keys, their cash, their tickets, their passports, their phones, even their underwear have vanished. When Abi snaps the handset closed, we all stare gravely at one another. Abi is the first to giggle. Her mouth parts slowly over her perfect row of teeth and she sniggers. Very slowly, we all mirror this deed; a sneer from Becky then a titter from Dee. Catherine snorts. Suddenly we're all screaming with laughter, the bags limp in our hands. 'You've got to haven't you?' Abi says. 'They even nicked their bloody pants!' On the other side of the gate families are eating their pre-prepared picnics. Young women with belly button rings and tattoos on the small of their backs walk around in fluorescent bikini tops. Young men smoke joints. Toddlers grizzle from beneath their sun umbrellas, ice-cream melting in their fists. We collapse on a spare patch of grass, a heap of fair skin, grocery bags and cellulite, eleven red faces emerging at the top. We play pass the parcel with a plastic water bottle refilled with vodka and blether about the steroid freak from Tonypandy who bit his girlfriend's nose off. By the time the headlining band are due on stage, Emily has taken to simply swishing her gypsy skirt aside and pissing out of the side of her knickers gusset. Catherine and I are still walking to the trees surrounding us and crouching behind a trunk. It's already dusk amongst the foliage. Toilet roll of all colours is strewn around the entire forest floor and somewhere in the background someone is singing, 'If you go down to the woods today....'

I actually bought the Super Furry Animals' first album, *Fuzzy Logic,* in 1996 because it was the most satisfying of the Brit Pop offerings. It had a wonderful little toe-tapper called

'Something for the Weekend'. 'First time did it for the hell of it, stuck it on the back of my tongue and swallowed it.' The album cover had photographs of Howard Marks and our national weather girl, Siân Lloyd, on its sleeve; symbols of home amongst a music scene saturated by Manchester. But over the looming decade their candy-coloured fusion of techno, psychedelia and pop became lost on me. The world had turned its attention to hip hop and rock and from that distance I regarded the Super Furry Animals as mere acid heads, trite and over-reliant on computer-generated samples. Of course nobody actually agreed with me. Everybody I knew loved them and the band went on to refine and extend their sound over five albums, the last of which included an entirely Welsh vocal. That's how I ended up here and two songs into the set I've fallen in love with them too. The lyrics are wry and comical, the tunes familiar. My legs turn weak when their performance climaxes with a tape loop of Bill Hicks proclaiming that 'all governments are liars and murderers,' and images of Bush and Blair fill the screens. The band launch into their profane, lefty anthem, 'The Man Don't Give a Fuck', armed with 52 F-bombs. Nowadays, very few bands express political opinions; indeed they are discouraged from it – isolating fans of opposite persuasions means losing sales. The last rock band to challenge this brand of authority was Rage against the Machine in the early 90s – the name says it all. The Super Furry Animals' have a clause written into their record contract which stipulates that members of the armed forces will not get their usual discount when they buy an album by the band. Recently, they turned down a seven-figure offer to sell their music to a worldwide Coca Cola advert. It's commendable and I immediately regret not pursuing the band as material for my book. My friends had always been quick to mention them – everyone had some sort of dubious link to them; somebody's uncle fixed a washing machine for the woman who lived next door to one of their grandparents. At least then I might have been in the VIP area sipping Pimm's with Kate Moss and Pete Doherty, instead of trying to urinate in the middle of the field, guarded from prying eyes by a circular wall of girlfriends. This gush of new found admiration however, may only be the effects of what I put on the back of my tongue several hours ago. It's hard to tell.

On our way back to our B&B I get déjà vu and then realise it's because we've walked past a pub called The Pump House, where Accidental Genocide played more than a decade ago. The memory of loading amplifiers into the back of a hired transit van and then trying to sleep on top of them while the driver bombed down the M4 revisits me like a warning. Now there are only six days to go. Suddenly, Becky decides that at 2am it's too early to retire. We plough back into the city centre, scouring the side streets for late opening pubs. Eventually we stumble into a nightclub, at the entrance of which we have to pass under an airport-style metal detector, get our bags checked for obscure weapons and get our chewing gums confiscated. Then we queue up at a till and pay £10 for the privilege. Inside the auditorium hundreds of people stand facing the stage, their arms punching the air, some of them holding mini light sabres, others blowing referee whistles. When the man in front of me moves out of the way I catch sight of the stage and there's nothing there; a DJ deck with a man standing behind it. Quickly I convince Emily to leave with me. 'You don't want to be listening to this dance music,' I tell her. 'It can cause brain disease, like police communication masts. And someone's bound to step on your feet in those delicate little heels.' We wait in a taxi rank for a lift back to Redland, a gang of eighteen-year-olds behind us with vomit stains on their T-shirts trying to work out if we're from Eastern Europe or Cornwall.

Riding in Cars with Boys

My mobile phone plays a Beatles tune, 'Paperback Writer' (cheesy, I know). I flick the hand-set open. Scott tells me that he and Gavin will be picking me up from my house in an hour. It's the first day of tour. I rush downstairs and prepare breakfast, which is really only instant coffee. Corporeal morning nourishment was replaced years ago by nicotine. I open the giant hold-all which has been standing to attention in the hall for two days. I force my last minute luggage inside; a bumper tub of petroleum jelly which I use to moisten my lips. (What the cosmetic industry doesn't tell you when it advertises its lip-gloss is that repeated overuse will result in your mouth being unable to produce its own moisture and you'll need either to use balms for the remainder of your life or sit tight through a two-month, dry-mouth cold-turkey. Everyone who has met me wonders why I'm smearing something transparent over my chin every couple of minutes, and this is why.) I have become the sum of all my addictions. I also pack tampons. Fate has decided to deal me one last blow. My period's a week early.

I feed the cat and put the television on. There are twenty-five music channels on a basic digital package, something I would have maimed for when I was sixteen and had to stay up until 2am on a school night, just to see a Metallica video. But simply having more of something doesn't necessarily make it better. I still have to stay up late to catch a real gem. One of the videos on high rotation today is a falsetto cover of Sparks' 'This Town Ain't Big Enough for the Both of Us'. It's Justin Hawkins' solo project. Frankie has recently left The Darkness. It's an acrimonious split but its exact reason is undisclosed. Three hours pass and I watch the video until the song's tune begins to sound like it's playing backwards. Justin's voice jars on me.

Finally, my telephone rings again. 'Come out on your door,' Scott says. 'We're late as fuck and there's no fucking street names in this place.' Outside, he's getting out of the passenger seat of a burgundy Fiat, his big hair fixed with lacquer, his black sunglasses obscuring his eyes. He takes my hold-all from me and carries it across the terraced street, throwing it in the boot of the car. I go back inside for my handbag and the big box of lager. He smiles wryly at it as he holds the bucket seat back for me to climb into the rear. 'I thought the Rhondda started and ended in Porth,' he says, 'I didn't know it came up this bloody far.' Gavin, the bass player, is sitting at the steering wheel, his sweatshirt sleeves rolled up on his tattooed forearms. 'Alright?' he says, nodding, and before I get chance to answer he turns the stereo up; 'Caffeine Bomb' by the Wildhearts. We screech out of the street and past the comprehensive school where the female fifth formers loiter through their last lunch break of the summer term. I sense my neighbours watching from behind their net curtains, wondering what the hell I'm doing. 'That's right,' I think, 'I'm riding in cars with boys.'

At the queue for the traffic lights in Treorchy there's time to point out my brother's tattoo studio with its giant body-jewellery display in the plate glass window. It looks impressive but I know his girlfriend made it with last year's left over Christmas trimmings. Gavin turns the radio down and leans back to look at me, his short, ginger hair, dyed black, tufts of peroxide curling up behind his ears. 'Will he do mates rates?' he says. Scott's on his phone, telling a mystery caller that he's picking up 'this journalist girl who's writing a book thing on the band.' 'My ex,' he says, as he flips the phone shut.

In Pontypridd we take the third exit at the roundabout outside Ynysangharad Park, merging onto the motorway; out of my valley and into theirs. I can vaguely remember school trips to Merthyr where at eight or nine years old we were taken on underground tours of the Cyfarthfa ironworks wearing hardhats that slipped down over our foreheads. There was one frail kid, the son of a projectionist at the Parc & Dare theatre, who always took fried egg sandwiches on these once-a-term minibus journeys and who always vomited on the teacher. In the castle we stood in front of portraits of the Crawshay family, stern-faced dead people in stiff Victorian collars, while we giggled over the specks of orange bile still clinging to Mrs Hughes' skirt. In the mid 19th century the town's iron production was the most important manufacturing concern on earth. We all know the story. Now, less than two hundred years later, Merthyr hosts the lowest life expectancy in Wales. Its children have the unhealthiest teeth in the UK.

20.5% of the town's population receive incapacity or sickness benefit. Unemployment, despite recent rises, stands at a whopping 63.5%.

As an adult I had only been into Merthyr on two occasions. Aged nineteen I changed trains at Pontypridd and headed for the industrial park which houses the famous red-brick Hoover factory, and onto the Simbec hospital in the hope of selling my body to science. The hospital was hosting the final stages of research into new pain-killing drugs. Before a product is launched it needs to be tested for safety on humans. Pharmaceutical conglomerates pay up to two thousand pounds a week for participation in their investigations. I needed money to complete my course at Glamorgan University and lying in a hospital bed with my writing pad on my lap while a nurse came by once in a while to administer and monitor the pills seemed a whole lot easier than working the twilight shift in a factory. There were a pile of forms on a desk in the foyer with a statement printed at the top: 'I have never had unprotected sex in sub-Saharan Africa.' The receptionist told me to sign it. A nurse guided me to an examination room where she took various samples of blood and hooked my pulse to a VDU, sticking cold, gelled pads in a range of vicinities around my near-naked body. When I'd dressed, a doctor came in and tested my responses by hitting my kneecaps with what looked like a bass drum pedal, something which up until that point I'd only ever seen on *Casualty*. A week later the hospital sent me a letter saying I was too thin to help them with their studies. I didn't think very much about it afterwards but whenever I visit my GP and he opens my medical file, I see the Simbec logo amongst the letterheads. It reminds me of the extent of my poverty and it makes me feel sick. In 2001, when I was twenty-two, a group of comprehensive school kids who were studying my novel invited me to a question and answer session. The school was on the Gurnos, a housing estate situated a mere fifteen minute drive away from Scott's house, an area notorious for poverty and crime. Some of the news stories spanning the past decade include accounts of drugs and murder. Perhaps the most infamous is that of Annette Hewins, Donna Clarke and Denise Sullivan. The three women, sometimes referred to as the Gurnos three, were wrongly convicted of an arson attack on the home of Diane Jones, aged 21, in October 1995. Someone had torn away part of the covering of her front door and poured in petrol to start the fire, supposedly an act of revenge for a love affair involving the victim's partner. The fire spread so rapidly that Ms Jones and her two daughters, Shauna, aged two, and Sarah-Jane, aged 13 months, were all killed. The convictions were quashed at the Court of Appeal in 1998 and the murders remain unsolved. More recently, in September 2004, a gang of twelve drug dealers who openly sold heroin and crack cocaine on the estate were sentenced to a total of seventy-one years in prison. They included Pauline Seal, a mother of four. Her children also received thirty-one years between them. Early in 2006, a former nurse pleaded guilty to concealing the birth of three of her own children following the discovery of babies' remains in two attics on the estate. Ann Mahoney, 63, went on trial later that month. On the Gurnos, nobody asked me why my Valleys-set writing (often about rape, paedophilia, poverty and attempted suicide, and blackmail, drugs of all classes, domestic violence, prostitution and death) was so dark. This was life as council estate Merthyr knew it.

Nowadays, Darran and I drive regularly along the A470, to

the supermarket on Dowlais Trading Estate where we buy our weekly groceries. There, it's easy to see the past, the present and the future of the town: it's a panoramic vista of natural green field beaten ugly by the brute force of industry. There's an assembly of terraced houses clinging to the edge of the valley like lumps of pastry mix in a bowl waiting to be washed, while in the foreground is a brand new retail park, replete with a huge advertising board on which a sinister Colonel Sanders grins. Looming large in the background is the bleak, grey stone of Merthyr's heritage. The clash of past and present, industrial and post-industrial, closing factories and opening superstores; a lesson in the relentless march of global capitalism and the people who are its perennial losers. But today we drive to Troedyrhiw via Abercynon, the white arches that mark the graves of the one hundred and sixteen children who died in the 1966 Aberfan disaster standing high on the flanking mountainside. The village is a virtual ghost town served by a lone shop, a surgery, a chemist. The neon yellow paint daubed on the bricks of a nearby terraced house puts me in mind of something I read in a national tabloid last Sunday: The first soldiers into Saddam Hussein's palace were Welsh Guardsmen. One of them looked at the gold-plated taps fixed to the pink bathroom suite and said, 'Jeez boys, it looks like someone from Merthyr Tydfil won the jackpot.'

Close to our destination Gavin shifts in his seat again to face me. 'You're okay for female company anyway, Rach,' he says. 'There's another girl coming. We don't know her really. She's something to do with the keyboard player.'

'Good,' I say, although I'm not really sure if it is. Many of my friends have teased me about spending the summer sleeping on a bus with a gang of rock musicians. There are temptations posed by this scenario, at least for me there are. Darran's made me swear pledges. My defence has been that it's work, something I cannot evade. 'I can't help being a girl,' I said. Of course, there's much more to it than that. I'm not sure if I want to share the uniqueness of being female with somebody else, it compromises my potential power. When he pulls against a kerb and runs into his house to retrieve the course of antibiotics treating his eczema, Scott says, 'Yeah, this girl we don't really know; I think Gav wants to screw her.' Three streets later, Gavin parks the Fiat, fiddling with the crook lock. Scott carries my lager and my pillow and I follow, dragging my ruck-sack along the pavement. It's filled with jeans, T-shirts and a week's supply of cigarettes. Now I'm thinking I should have packed a dress, or at least a toothbrush and a bottle of shampoo.

Bands in Vans

The arse end of the bus they call 'Black Betty', is sticking out
of a driveway, slate grey clouds puffing noxiously out of her
exhaust. Inside, the band members sit around a collapsible
table. Chris looks up from beneath his straight, black fringe,
regarding me warily. Matt's frowning, eager to leave. The skin
of his face is clear and smooth like a chubby baby's. Two
spiked studs shoot out at either side of his bottom lip like
the metal teeth of a warthog. I smile apologetically at him but
even as I do I feel smug for holding the tour up. (It must be
an overhang from my time with Accidental Genocide.) The girl
wears a pink fitted jacket, her dark hair tied up in a pony-tail.
It's impossible to tell how old she is, but she's pretty and
younger than me. She has a beauty spot lip-piercing sitting on
her thick top lip. I sit next to Dan, the sound technician from
Cardiff Barfly who they're paying £10 a day. He has a mop of
brown curly hair and sits easily with his arm balanced on the

bench cushion behind me. 'Dan's French,' Scott says. The pine table top is filled with black felt-tip graffiti; band names and crass diagrams of easy women, their legs splayed open, their feet and hands oversized. Scott, who seems concerned about my first impression, points at one of the childish scribbles. 'That's what Gav thinks a cunt looks like,' he says. He rolls his eyes and sits on the box of lager, protecting it like a hen. Matt reaches his foot underneath him and jabs the box, as if to check it's real.

I spy into the bedroom where there are two sets of bunks on either wall. The pillow and the duvet covers are all made out of the same material – cotton marine camouflage print. Books and bags and clothing are strewn across the mattresses. I'd never been on a tour bus that had proper sleeping compartments before. In band interviews, when the band members mentioned their buses, it always sounded decadent that they had this life away from home; another bed, away from their bed, where all the secret things happened. I'm aware suddenly that one of my teenage dreams is coming true but the timing is somewhat belated and at sixteen I could never have imagined that it could remind me of sleepovers at my cousin's. The whole bus smells like boy. We reverse into the street where Matt's mother is standing, waving anxiously.

'Can I smoke then?' the girl says, producing her packet of ten Lambert & Butler.

Scott stands up and opens the skylight. When he gets down he taps the box of lager, looking at me as though the girl's request has given him the strength to abandon his refinement. I nod and wave my hand around the table. 'Let's all have one.' Alcohol is my preferred method of ice-breaking.

'If you *are* going to smoke, Beth,' Gavin says, 'you'll have to give me a fag. Rules are rules.' He stares unflinchingly at her. She grimaces, showing him the inside of the silver box where there's only one cigarette left.

Scott passes the bottles around. I pass mine back and take a brown bottle of Warsteiner out of my handbag. 'That's some connoisseur shit,' he says, looking at the German label. I yank the top off with my key chain bottle-opener and simultaneously light a cigarette. I pass one to Gavin.

'See?' he says, glaring at Beth.

Beth ignores him. 'What shall I use as an ashtray?' she says.

'You can have this now,' Scott says. He toasts her with his bottle and downs the contents in one. He puts the empty in the centre of the table where depending on which way the bus turns, either Beth or Gavin have to stop it sliding off the surface. Scott points at the Corona box, silently asking for another.

Above us, a plastic grocery bag full of vinegar and sauce sachets hangs from the ceiling. Gavin pulls it down and empties the contents over the table. He explains how he stole them from a service station last week because it was late at night and there was nothing edible left to take. He separates the sachets into various piles. The mayonnaise represents twenty, the brown sauce, ten, the vinegar, five – condiment poker. 'This is as exciting as it gets,' he says. 'Playing?'

'I'm not playing,' Scott says. 'Iss numbers isn' i?'

I decline for the same reason.

On a roundabout on the Heads of the Valleys road, a boy runs towards the bus, a foil-wrapped sandwich in a plastic bag rolled up in his fist. He's skinny and fair-haired, his face plastered with freckles. He looks like Huckleberry Finn in his cut-off combat trousers; only the stem of straw is missing. 'Alright Rach?' he says, as though we've met before. It's Lyndon, the keyboard player. He sits down and reaches into a partition in the wall behind him where an iPod is lying idle. He turns it on. Mötley Crüe comes throbbing out of the concealed speakers; definitive party music, for those who like to rock.

The driver puts his foot down in an attempt to complete the four hour journey in two and make the sound-check scheduled for 3.30. I notice this month's *Rock Sound* magazine, in which Midasuno are highlighted, rolled up and stuffed into the wedge between the table and the window. I unfurl it and search for the article, quarter of the way in. It's a whole page, a part of the magazine's regular feature titled 'Bands in Vans'. There's a suitable monochrome picture of Midasuno, their faces staring out above their black T-shirts. I look at them slowly, first checking the real faces around me and then the faces in the magazine, from left to right, like a teacher trying to memorise her pupils on the first day of class. Chris Morgan, the puny kid opposite me, wears the same Ramones T-shirt as today. Scott Andrews, as though he always has his mind on the future's main chance, looks directly at the camera. Matt Riste is laughing, his cheeks split into dimples. Lyndon Jones is about to speak, the Crüe of the Mötley Crüe only just visible behind his black hoody, his mouth forming around a new word. Gavin Jessop's got a tight-lipped smirk embedded in his features, his eyes opened wide; mischievous and joker-like. I look up from the magazine to see him standing in front of the windscreen, his jeans forced down his thighs as he moons the car in front. The driver tells me that this is nothing, he stripped naked for a photo-shoot recently when the photographer complained that her work with bands always looked too 'samey'. I look down at the magazine – they're all here. I read the article, all about

Midasuno's determination to release their album – their sacrifices with beer-money and girlfriends – when I come across something quite coincidental. I have to stop and reread the sentence. 'Their first option,' it says, 'was to sell their bodies to medical research, spend a few months in the hands of the NHS and use the money to cover the expenses of their album.' Simbec! It's another of those happenstances that cement my fledgling relationship with the band. We share a certain quality and it's called defiance: blind defiance.

'Is it alright?' Matt says, gesturing at the magazine.

'Yeah, fine.'

The bus enters the Newport tunnel, heading eastbound on the M4, and the band open their mouths and moan a doctor surgery style 'aaaaghh' for the length of it; an old tour tradition. I hand the magazine to Beth who's waiting for it. She flicks backwards until she gets to an article on The Subways and points female bass player Mary-Charlotte Cooper out to Lyndon. 'I'd shag her,' she says.

We're an hour away from our destination when Dan gets up and stands at the open door of the moving bus, screaming at passing cars. 'Get your rat out,' he shouts, his French accent fluently locking the words of this obscure sexual reference together, the wind thrashing his curls about. Scott and Gavin piss straight out onto the hard shoulder. I at least get the driver to pull up before I ramble behind a holly bush and peel my jeans down. I lose my balance as I tuck my tampon string back into my knickers, simultaneously catching myself, one hand pressed against the grass verge. It's four in the afternoon, and the party has already started.

Til Death Do Us Party

Beth and I are sitting in the empty first floor bar, watching the band do their sound check; unsure of conversation topics. I discovered her age when on arrival she turned around in the gangway of the women's lavatory, showing me the buttocks of her light blue jeans and asked if she was 'showing' – schoolgirl language designed to detect blood stains, suggestive of form five cigarette breaks. In my school, when the answer was yes, the solution was a wad of rough, recycled toilet paper stuffed up your navy skirt. My body has lost this youthful ability to shock me so suddenly. By your late twenties you know the flow of your menstrual cycle better than you know yourself, even when you're early, you know how your tits swell up like over-ripe cantaloupe melons, and you know what absorbency you should use. I'm not sure that anything I have to say is relevant to Beth and I'm starting to feel like a spare prick in a wedding when the promoter approaches with his rubber stamp.

'Have you paid, girls?' he says. His name is Steve Hawkins; a former sound technician, painfully thin and camp as a row of pink tents. He's one of the band's favourite promoters. He feeds them properly, lets them use his own shower. I tell him I'm a journalist. Beth says she's the merchandise girl. You can buy T-shirts now, the simple phrase, *I'm with the Band*, embroidered across the bust. I should have brought one. 'It's always the same,' he says, throwing his arms into the air, theatrically. 'Nobody ever wants to effing pay.'

We're in a venue called the Bivouac, on the outskirts of Lincoln. Squat, red-brick houses rotate in spirals around us. Teenagers wearing Burberry baseball caps loiter in bus stops. It's ironic that this is the international denominator for chav culture. The Burberry factory sits on wasteland at the top of Treorchy, two miles away from my house. My uncle was the human resources manager there until he died of lung cancer, aged fifty-five. Victoria Beckham and Beyonce are not aware of the factory's location it seems, when they buy their shopping bags from Harrods or their bikinis from Rodeo Drive boutiques. The uneducated working class kids, the 'chavs' who want to look like them, aren't aware of the factory either, but I like to think they are somehow, and that what they're actually doing is deliberately reclaiming the red, white and beige checker of Burberry back for themselves. A door at the side of the stage leads into the promoter's house, a maze of carpet-less corridors where an Alsatian dog lies sleeping. Midasuno's dressing room is an abandoned bedroom clogged with stacks of pub chairs and clean ashtrays. On the damp walls there are dusty photographs of kids with basin haircuts; children who have long grown up. A wallpaper pasting table pushed up against the windowsill tries to disguise itself under a picnic blanket. On it sit various loaves of bread, blocks of cheese and dishes of fruit and salad. A crate of Kronenbourg balances on the seat of a chair.

Gavin sits opposite me and we start talking about tattoos again. I take my shoe off, peel my sock to my toes and show him my latest addition; a sea-green tribal butterfly perched on the front of my right foot – the universal symbol for progress, lovingly engraved by the hand of my big brother. Eventually I'll get around to adding the text: *Just when the caterpillar thought the world was about to end, it turned into a butterfly.* I have to find an abbreviation that fits.

'Didn't it hurt?' he says. That's what everybody says. He tells me the Lord's Prayer story: rumour has it that if you get the Lord's Prayer tattooed on the sole of your foot, you can walk into any tattoo studio in the world and demand free work. Of course you could if you could first brave the pain of a needle pressing holes into the skin meant to protect your nerve endings; there isn't a local anaesthetic strong enough to numb it, and secondly, if the tattoo ever healed intact: movement and sweat would prevent it. He lifts his sleeve and looks at his arm. He wants one of Chris' belt buckles reproduced above his elbow. He nods at what's already there and says, 'I don't know why I got those done,' meaning the fading, red, five-sided stars on the inside of his forearm, 'probably because my girlfriend told me to.' None of the others have tattoos but Matt is considering a modern adaptation of a classic: 'love' and 'hate' above his knuckles; the characters: Old English script.

Dan and Chris leave to search for the nearest off licence and buy supplies for the night ahead. I look around at the woodchip wallpaper, feigning interest.

'This,' Gavin says, 'is as exciting as it gets.' It's the second time he's said it. He's obviously trying to hide something so I laugh and ask him what it is. For my perception I'm rewarded with a batch of good, old fashioned rock 'n' roll tour stories, like the time they walked into a High Wycombe pub to ask where they should load their gear in, only to see a naked pole dancer on the stage.

'I shit you not,' Scott says, joining in. 'Saturday afternoon, the football hadn't even started.' Very quickly, the subject matter gets personal. 'This is off the record,' Gavin says. It's the code-phrase we've chosen to remind me, in no uncertain terms, to switch the interview off. Being this close to the band is like a sex game where 'no' could easily mean 'yes'. Anything other than 'this is off the record', could be ambiguous. Gavin looks relieved and the tension clouding the atmosphere dissolves like a deciphered illusion. I'm disappointed. I want to document everything. But we're only a day into the tour. Pretty soon they're going to forget I'm even here.

Lyndon bursts into the room, a grin spanning his face. He picks a loaf of bread up, ripping it in two. 'Bet you can't eat this sandwich I make for you,' he says, gouging the dough out, and leaving it, like rubbish, on the banquet table. 'Come on Gav, you eat this and I'll buy you a drink at the bar.' He tears cherries from their stalks and drops them into the empty hunk followed by chunks of banana, cucumber, onion and slices of apple. He spoons thick daubs of mayo out of its jar and drops them into the sandwich, then passes it to Gavin. Gavin looks at me apprehensively before biting into the bread. He's still chewing when Matt comes in with a baseball bat he's found behind the stage. He looks like a heavy, threatening us, slapping the bat against his palm. He says he's found a bloke in the crowd, an

Andrew something, who's just bought my book; at least he thinks it's my book because the bloke says it has the Childline telephone number printed in the back. Speaking as he is, in a strange and equivocal code, it's difficult to decipher what he's driving at, so I say nothing. Lyndon, who's next to me, leans over. 'Did you really write a whole book?' he asks. It reminds me of a story Welsh poet, Dannie Abse, told me at his 80th birthday party. He'd been trying to get his young son interested in his writing career; pulling books off the shelves and explaining that Daddy had written them. One afternoon his son was playing with a classmate in the study. Abse was eavesdropping from behind the door. His son struggled to drag one of the books from the top shelf and carry it over to his friend. 'See this big book?' he said. 'Yes,' his friend said. 'My mother typed it all.' Scott breaks the silence in the room when he opens the window and aims an orange into the courtyard. Dan is returning, another crate of lager cradled to his chest, and the fruit hits him on his crown. The band cheers triumphantly, jumping over the stacks of chairs, rushing towards the window.

I watch the show from the comfort of the merchandise stall. The cabaret tables around me are occupied by thirty-something couples. The men are overweight; their round bellies pushing out of thrash metal T-shirts. The women drink shorts; talking loudly with thick Northern accents. The dance floor is half-filled with twenty-somethings standing solemnly at the front of the stage, watching the boys pummel their instruments like it's their last night with fingers. Beth approaches me several times during the set and asks me to join her on the dance floor. When I refuse, shaking my head politely, she frowns perplexedly and walks dejectedly back into the crowd. The band's contact list is Sellotaped to the surface of the table

97

in front of me, three-quarters full of handwritten e-mail addresses; every one a person waiting for their next newsletter. The black T-shirts are folded in neat rows beside it, the Midasuno logo printed across the bust area in red with an insignia underneath which says, 'Til Death Do Us Party.' Midasuno claim to be a 'party' band: average boys who grew up on the breadline admiring the debauched behaviour of their idols. They have nothing to lose. 'We've never shied away from a night out,' Scott told me once, 'but a tour is a fair fucking few nights out on the trot and there's little time for fucking about. It could all end tomorrow, so live it like you mean it.' Their heroes are my heroes. This is the closest I'm going to get to being backstage at Wembley Stadium with Guns 'n' Roses and I suppose I've come to see this travelling orgy of over-indulgence in action; to refute or confirm the myth, and if I can confirm it, write myself into it – be the Allen Ginsberg on Bob Dylan's 1975 Rolling Thunder Revue, the Tori Amos baking the chicken in the Nine Inch Nails recording studio. This is my humble shot at legendary, being and telling.

John is sitting next to me, smiling. He's Matt's father and Midasuno's tour manager and bus driver; a big man with grey salt and pepper hair clipped close to his skull and a pair of greying weight-lifter's pants. 'You must have a lot of faith in them,' I say, 'to spend your entire life driving them around.' He says he's been driving them around since they were eight then he continues to smile genially, his eyes focused on the performance he's already seen a thousand times. The band are about to complete their set, Scott thanking the audience. 'We're going to be at the Arts Centre in Worcester tomorrow,' he says, 'and while we're there we'll check out Fred West's house.' I must remind him later that Fred West's house was in Gloucester but had been demolished a decade ago. They throw their instruments to the floor and disappear amid a cacophony of reverb, leaving the crowd applauding. 'Now I have to do my other job,' John says, and he hobbles to the stage and dismantles Matt's faux-fur leopard-print covered drum kit, his ever-present NHS crutches hanging from his forearms. Despite his limp, there is no physical evidence of their necessity. It's a bizarre sight which tells as much about life in Merthyr as Scott's acerbic lyrics.

Back on the bus, my appetite for alcohol has fallen by the wayside. Sometime during the age it took to trawl the gear down the stairs, the Friday night chill has crept into my bones and my epiglottis got lazy. I tell Scott that I have to go to sleep and his face cracks from post-gig swell to an unhappy pattern of concern. He steps into the bedroom, tidying his quilt up, offering me his bunk. It's the bottom one on the left. I get fully clothed onto his mattress and arrange myself around his belongings; his paperbacks are stacked under his pillow, his laptop is under my feet and I lie like a smile, bowing in the middle. The others are nominating their 'prick of the day'. It's a bonding exercise they've conjured specifically for this tour. I think I've got away with it when Lyndon pops his head into the bedroom demanding my participation. 'You've got to,' he says, adamantly, his bob-length, mousey hair tucked behind his ears. I think about who I least want to offend. Eventually I nominate Dan with suitably lame reasoning – he's French. Another round of nominations follows, this time for 'Man of the Match'. Gavin is citing me for my endless supply of cigarettes when the bus starts moving. The wind whistles passed my left ear canal so I bunch the cold, stale quilt against it until something akin to sleep seizes me.

Along Came Mong

The waste bin beside me is overflowing with cigarette packets and cardboard coffee cups. It all spews out around my socks. The ashtray at the top is full of cellophane and cigarette butts. Nicotine has bled into the thin layer of dew coating the steel base, turning it putrid and ginger. I stub out my second. I woke at nine, still on civilian time, my bladder expanding into my torso. I swung my legs out of the bunk and was about to plant them on the floor when I saw Matt underneath me, laid out on sponge cushions, his bulk taking up the whole width and length of the aisle, like a giant baby in a giant cot. Somehow I transported myself into the living area of the bus without actually touching him, where there were four more bodies to circumvent; indistinct lumps of black denim in a sea of mismatched bed linen. John was sitting in the driver's seat, a white continental quilt bunched up around him. He opened his eyes and quickly searched for the door's release. It opened with a puff.

Opposite me, people file in and out of another big automatic door, beneath a sign which says 'Tamworth Services', their sleep-creased faces the same sallow, yellow colour as the brickwork. I heard a comedian comment once that motorway service stations were an industry founded on a man who wanted a shit. This is untrue, obviously, because a motorway service station is possibly the most uncomfortable place in the universe to have a shit (and that includes a downtrodden nest of stinging nettles in a three-day rave in a field in Chepstow). It's an industry, founded, like all industries, on attempts to part fools with their money. There's a Burger King here, an M&S, a Coffee Republic, a newsagent, a man selling insurance, a coin-slot massage couch and a wide collection of video games whose mechanised blip-blip noises are beginning to chew at the edges of my headache. And yet, no act of consumption can fully mask the famished sensation of an incomplete road journey. Customers trawl out, their eyes the same bored, unfulfilled holes they were when they entered. A middle-aged woman in a denim jacket, the heads of two miniature Yorkshire terriers poking out of either breast pocket, sits down beside me on the cold wrought iron bench.

The bus is parked in the back corner of the lorries' overnight section, presumably as far away from the service building as John could possibly get it. Sweat sparkles on her rippling black body. Some of the others are awake; I can hear them stirring but I sit on a kerb in the car park and wait. Gavin materialises first. He pisses on the bus's rump, readjusts his studded white leather belt so his marl boxershorts balloon out of the top, just so, and then he lies on the tarmac beside me. I give him a cigarette and we smoke in easy silence, not thinking anything. Around us, parked cars begin to accumulate and we watch a Ford pull up in the empty space opposite. A couple in tailored clothes alight. The woman looks condescendingly at Gavin as he inattentively scratches his white belly. Her eyes are so full of loathing I have to turn and look at Gavin to deduce what offends her so much. I stare at him for a moment but I can't work out what it is. He looks like a boy, not exceptionally handsome or extraordinarily unattractive, tall and rough around the edges, but mostly just a boy, like all of the other boys from the Valleys I've looked at and never noticed. Another car and another couple arrive. This woman too squints unhappily at us. They all seem to know each other, these people who resent us so deeply; they chat with English middle-class accents while they unfasten their seatbelts and lift their offspring out. I've lost interest in them, when, after a minute, they all drive off again.

'Did you see that?' Gavin says. 'They swapped kids! They just swapped their fucking kids.' The potential motives for exchanging children on a Saturday morning in an anonymous car park in a corner of nowhere, although probably existent, are momentarily quite difficult to grasp, so I shrug. Gavin yawns and stretches, his fists punching the air.

A few hours later, we're on our way to Worcester, sitting on the benches around the collapsible table, in the same position as yesterday. Chris, Beth, Lyndon and Matt are opposite, Gavin's beside me. Today we are drained of pre-tour energy. The bus has taken on the collective mood of a tired delinquent. Dan stands and wordlessly heads into one of the empty bunks, pushing past Scott who sits in the gangway, staring at the floor. Beth mutely rummages around in her cosmetic bag for a lighter. Despite three head counts, all of which add up to nine, I can't help thinking that there are people missing. The official capacity of the bus is thirteen and initially there were worries about fitting me on. There's a magazine on the table, opened to a quarter page advertisement for the tour, the black ticker tape dates pressed against the red silhouette of a woman's ecstatic face. I start reading the text, oblivious to where it's taking me. 'The Midsummer Murder Tour,' it says, 'with very special guests...' That's it – there's a whole band missing. 'Where's your support band?' I ask suddenly.

'They've got their own transit van,' Matt says. 'The Pop Factory hired it.'

The Pop Factory is a television studio in the Rhondda. Avanti, the company responsible for much of the Stereophonics' live footage, and formally based in an upmarket Cardiff suburb, moved its production facilities into the Corona pop factory at the gateway to the valley with the aid of a massive pre-Millennium grant, borne by Objection One funding. The purpose of the money spilling out of the EU coffers was to go some way to improving the poorest areas of Wales, the South Wales Valleys being the biggest of them. And at a time when the manufacturing industry was quickly thinning, but Welsh pop music was increasingly successful, the emergence of a venture making claims to train and employ local people in the art of music making and recording seemed like a perfectly sound idea. The building had been derelict for over twenty years; I have only very vague memories of the soft drinks it used to produce – a tasteless fizz which came in a multitude of colours from the lorry that roamed the valley on a Friday afternoon. My Nanna had two bottles of dandelion & burdock every week and she got a few coppers back for returning the bottles. The new Pop Factory opened in 2000 when Tom Jones got out of a limo and smashed a bottle of champagne against the brickwork. The photographers from the local newspaper went nuts. And there it was, our phoenix emerging out of all the decaying shit.

Two years had passed when I began to wonder exactly what it was The Pop Factory did. Of course they filmed their weekly *Top of the Pops*-style show there, but I only got to see the interior of the building when it was televised on ITV. The list of famous band names rolling in and out of Porth was impressive but the role of the locals, it seemed, was simply to be the audience, to clap and dance and stand still on cue; exciting for a twelve-year-old though it may be, hardly life-affirming. Marcus Lawry's Poisoned Whiskey Records were still holed up in a function room in a nearby pub and to complicate things further, Elwa, Wales' tax-funded education body, awarded Avanti £4 million in 2002 to open an MP3 café in a derelict supermarket close to The Pop Factory site. It was intended to attract disengaged young people back to practical learning and would have web design, photography and mixing facilities. Later it would emerge from an official audit report that Elwa had paid out the money in advance to sit unused in Avanti's bank account, the premises yet to be renovated; people yet to be trained. I was sent by *The Big Issue* to interview the company on this matter. They nominated a slick, media-trained events organiser as their spokesperson. Pablo Janczur had worked for *Kerrang!* and *Q* magazine. He was a big man who wore a Hawaiian shirt and sat on the edge of the table, shuffling papers and answering his mobile while I spoke to him. He didn't know it, he didn't recognise me, but he'd thrown me out two months earlier for smoking in the television studio. He told me that the company were working with the Rhondda Cynon Taff Council and intended to bid for a new contract with Elwa; the MP3 café was scheduled to be up and running in summer 2004. When I pushed him on their lack of support for the local music community, he said that The Pop Factory was a business, a brand, 'like Coca Cola', and while he had no intention of closing the door on Valleys people, profit was chief. Following this, The Pop Factory inexplicably, but very gradually, opened its doors to the community. Poisoned Whiskey Records held gigs there on a room rental basis. So did Sonig, the Council's youth songwriting scheme. Perhaps because they had to unlock the building's earning potential, they occasionally hosted a live gig.

The Pop Factory is six years old now and anyone who wants to go inside the building can, providing they pay the entrance fee, but it still often seems as though it isn't there at all. I remember standing on the balcony on a freezing October evening, smoking, while Stuart Cable walked up the red carpet, towards the entrance, a D-List television presenter on his arm. (He'd win an award for the year's 'Most Rock 'n' Roll Excess'.) The camera beamed up to the press room was trained on the empty ceremony hall as guests began arriving. There were three tables at the front loaded with champagne flutes and flowers and favours and each of them had tickets folded into their centre-pieces which said, 'Reserved for the Rhondda Cynon Taff Council'. Outside, security guards stood behind the iron gates while local children thrust their arms through the balustrades, flagging them. One of the girls noticed me and shouted up. 'A, you, you skinny reporter bitch!' When she'd got my attention she smiled.

'Is Daniel Bedingfield in there?' she said. On the eve of this show I'd interviewed the winners of last year's 'Best Newcomers' award, Cardiff band Sammo Hung, trying to ascertain if the award had in any way made them successful since. Frontwoman Jemma Roper answered her telephone brusquely (I'd woken her up; she was working nights at the local TV aerial factory), and said, 'Nah, not really.' To all intents and purposes, Avanti looked like one of its own meaningless celebrities, pampering itself into believing it was exceptional.

The most recent winners of this newcomer award are a Neath/Swansea trio called Along Came Man. I know little about the band although I've heard recently they were booked as a support act when The Pop Factory hosted Tom Jones' 65th Birthday Concert, live from Ynysangharad Park in May 2005. I'd also read a small snippet of information published in the entertainment section of a local newspaper claiming that they were the first signing on The Pop Factory's new record label, and that the company had put them up in a house in Jenkin Street where they could write an album without the pressures of paying rent to distract them, the same street where those kids were trying to push through the barricades in search of their pop idols, a mere ten yards away from the still as yet unfinished MP3 café.

I look back at the magazine and continue reading, the bus's engine whirring. Pete's Sake was the support band for the previous leg of the tour. The Next Nine Years are the next. Above the current block of dates is Along Came Man, their band logo, sixties-style lowercase, shortened to one word. 'But why didn't they come on this bus?' I ask.

Matt opens his mouth but Scott jumps in first. 'We only invited them because we knew Kerys, their drummer. Then two weeks before tour, she left. She found out they'd been holding auditions for a new drummer behind her back, and secondly, they kept harassing me, demanding to know the sleeping arrangements.' He waves his arm around the bus, indicating the lack of formal sleeping arrangements. 'I told them I hadn't sorted it out yet but then Andrew got his knickers in a twist and started ringing the other boys.'

'Andrew?' I say, remembering that the name of the guy with a copy of my novel had been Andrew. 'Is that the same Andrew who bought my book?'

'Yeah,' Matt says. 'Trying to suck up to you.' He turns his attention to Scott and says, 'When you do your thank you at the end of set, you should say, "I'd like to thank Along Came Men." It's subtle. Let's see if they notice.' I lean forward in my seat, intrigued by Matt's dislike for the support band. If Scott agrees, there could be a fight.

'How about,' Scott says, smiling nefariously, 'I say, "I'd like to thank Along Came Mong?"'

The bus explodes into laughter. When it's quietened down, Scott, as though he's caught wind of my thought, looks straight at me. 'They're not playing tonight anyway,' he says, 'promoter didn't want them.'

Bright Pink Eye Shadow

Beth's cow-brown pupils peer up from the pages in her magazine. It's one of those glossy tabloid publications filled with colourful paparazzi pictures of celebrities who are famous for being celebrities, their pet shih-tzus clutched to their bosoms. We're on a lunch break, parked at the entrance of a Sainsbury's car park, the bus empty.

'Have you got a boyfriend?' she asks. I peel the cellophane back on my Ploughman's sandwich and pick at it while I tell her about my forthcoming wedding: the date, the location, the bridegroom, the Guns 'n' Roses cover band I want to play at the reception. (I discovered them at a local workingman's club where I reverted into a fourteen-year-old; stole onto the stage during their performance, nicked Slash's felt top hat, kissed Duff on the cheek and stage-dived off. I can remember the glint of pride in the bass player's eyes as I pecked him, as though he'd forgotten the peroxide blonde wig on his head and thought I actually fancied *him*.) 'Wow,' Beth says, in a way which suggests our understanding of marriage to be very different. She's thinking about the gown, the tiara, the bouquet, not about the commitment, the compromise; the actual betrothal. 'I split up with my boyfriend last week,' she says.

Gavin breezes onto the bus, signalling the end of our conversation. He puts a small, plastic pot on the table in front of him, a supermarket concoction of cold pasta and coleslaw. In the absence of a spoon he begins to eat it with the top right hand corner of his national insurance card. Beth jumps back into her magazine. In the distance I can see Dan leaving the shop, a large crate of lager in his trolley. He walks through the car park towards us, Scott beside him, laughing eagerly.

'Oh no,' I hear John whisper to himself from behind the curtain separating us. 'It isn't dinner time yet.' Dan has the day off because the Worcester venue has an in-house engineer but the band most definitely have to perform; they're the headline act. When they reach us, Dan begins unloading the cans. He passes me one, base first. Scott stays outside drinking, the tin tilted in the air. I can't see it but I guess John must be staring at him admonishingly. Scott holds the can away from him for a moment and says, 'What? It's only one. It'll wake me up.' It isn't long before Chris and Scott have Beth sitting inside the trolley, her eyes screwed closed with both hands clinging to the bars. They race her spinning around the car park, slops of lager jumping out of her can. When they hit the wing of a shiny new parked car, John promptly drives us all out of the vicinity, onto the motorway towards Worcester.

It's two o'clock when we arrive at the Arts Centre. John drops us off on the pavement and leaves to park the bus on the outskirts of the town. There is already a queue of teenagers in studded belts, filing along the High Street. They stand huddled in semi-circles, chatting, a mass of body jewellery, eyeliner and angst. More than a decade ago, I was doing exactly the same thing. Sunny Saturday afternoons were wasted sitting on the red metal benches in the Tonypandy Square bus stops, watching alcoholics stumble to and from the Pandy Inn, constantly re-applying my fire-engine-red lipstick, waiting for the doors of the Naval Club to open. But it was just me and one other school friend, a girl who, via the uncertain routes of Spandau Ballet and Meat Loaf, I'd bullied into listening to rock music. Our fellow gig-goers were fully formed adults from a distinctly different generation. Even on the streets of Nottingham I'd been the youngest patron in the guitar discos; the bouncers knew I was underage but they let me in because I never attempted to purchase alcohol, not personally at least. I'm not sure if I was a changeling or a throwback. The main difference between being into rock music then and being into rock music now is the number of people involved. The world is smaller and independent music is more accessible and the passion doesn't seem to have been diluted. Promoters have been quick to note the trend and clubs host under-eighteen live nights, Coca Cola on tap. The Pop Factory's is called *Teen Spirit*.

This is a similar set up, an all-day festival organised by Midasuno's former record label. It's been a while since they've parted company but the band is a big crowd puller in Worcester and has been invited, nonetheless. Inside the building the corridors are adorned with amateur watercolours. There are two stages, both ringed by spectators. One is acoustic. The other is the opposite of acoustic. Outside on the sun-drenched forecourt there's a burger bar and a merchandise stall. We stand beside the boot table, Matt coveting the rows of Misfits shoelaces. Scott sees somebody he recognises, a man in a baseball cap, his arms sleeved with fantasy-style tattoos. It's the kind of work that began small, but continued growing; virgin skin sacrificed for the addictive nature of body art. They wave and make towards each other, meeting on middle ground.

'Ben,' Gavin says, nudging me, 'a guy from the record company.' He raises his eyebrows, clearly irked, and pretends to take an interest in the CDs on sale in front of us. The red cover of *When Bulls Play God* stands out between the Clash box-sets. He prods it regretfully.

A little later, I'm with Scott. He needs new guitar strings and we're scouring the town for the local music shop. The pavements are teeming with Saturday shoppers who weave in and out of the arts, crafts and cake shops. We've sidestepped the main shopping area in favour of the small businesses surrounding the centre. The hardwood Tudor beams fixed to the first floor of the buildings remain intact. We're standing in front of the entrance to a cinema when Scott asks an elderly woman for help. She shakes her head and swiftly walks away. It is only then that I realise he's already wearing his full stage make-up. There are spheres of bright pink eye-shadow painted into the circumference of his eye sockets. His hair is backcombed and hardened with lacquer. Where this transformation happened exactly, it's hard to say. I imagine he did it in the van at some point between Tamworth and Worcester, already anticipating his public. There's a pine-frame Hyper Value mirror hooked to the wall behind Matt's seat but I'd failed to notice the actual application. The people of Worcester, however, have not. Adults look away as though they're ashamed for him. Children titter, and when we've passed, mutter jibes. I've always found men

112

who wear eye make-up utterly fascinating. (My initial interest in rock music coincided with my initial interest in cosmetics. I learned to apply my own make-up, not from the beauty pages of *Just Seventeen* but the promo photographs of glam rock bands.) This intrigue probably began much earlier though, aged something like six, watching Boy George or Pete Burns on *Top of the Pops*. Music is a form of entertainment pushing into the boundaries of costume drama. At its most basic, it's a disregard for gender stereotyping, as simple as a woman wearing jeans or drinking from a pint glass; a smack of rebellion. Aesthetically, I can think of nothing sexier and I smile wryly at the hail storm of conservatism aiming at us. Scott doesn't flinch. He doesn't even seem to notice.

The guitar shop is one of the last buildings on a street leading away from the centre of the town. The window is blocked by advertisements, handwritten on yellowing postcards: 'Hardcore punk band with record deal seeks vocalist, no time wasters', 'Experienced singer with own transport seeks band'. The guitars are hanging on rails, like suits. It smells of carpet tiles and central heating; a familiar and yet alien place which takes us out of the realms of mascara and highlights our differences rather than our similarities.

I've tried playing every musical instrument I've ever come into contact with, but for some reason, nothing stuck. There was violin at junior school, an excuse to avoid the playground at break-time, and then at fourteen my brother bought me an electric guitar. I took lessons but gave up when I got to bar chords, a surrender I've always deeply regretted, partly because there aren't enough women playing rock music. For a time I tried to compensate for my lack of musicality by listening to girl grunge band, L7. Gradually I realised that much of their material was lacklustre and I reverted back to an armchair enthusiast of male-orientated rock. It's a subservient position but a guilty pleasure; a subconscious form of pornography. In today's post-feminist climate there are ostensibly fewer obstacles for women to overcome. I generally ignore any gender stereotyping still hanging around. Rock music is the only medium in which I still feel inferior, but far from being an albatross, this feeling is often one of gratification. Sometimes I can't be bothered to go out and set fire to the world. Sometimes I want to put lipstick on and watch attractive men play their highly phallic guitars. Scott is the star here, I'm merely the observer. I self-consciously squint at the colourful plectrums, lined up in cases on the counter. When I had guitarist boyfriends I collected guitar picks. I caught one signed by Dimebag Darrell at a Pantera concert once. He was shot dead onstage in 2004 by a crazed fan, an incident likely to increase the plectrum's value. I make a mental search for it while Scott requests his strings.

Back at the Arts Centre, Matt stands alone at the entrance to the crowded basement. I'm not sure yet if it's a mark of respect or a cautious act designed to size the competition up, but this is usually where Matt is; his eyes fixed resolutely on the performances preceding his own. The room is muggy with the lukewarm pheromones of teenagers. There's a hardcore metal outfit on stage, playing their encore. The girl singer's low growl intersperses a discharge of sombre bass. It sounds like a Black Sabbath 7inch played backwards, as though she's pressing the microphone against her arse and farting into it. Matt, however, is clearly impressed.

'It's that band we played with once in Manchester,' he gasps. 'Hasn't her voice improved?' We climb the stairs, heading back out onto the forecourt, free of the auditorium's cloying atmosphere. His cheeks are flushed. 'I think I'm in love with her,' he says.

'Talk to her,' Scott says, with a paternal inflection I've never heard before, 'and tell her *I* love her hair.' He turns to me to explain his hair isn't big enough; he needs hairspray to style it. He's about to leave when the girl Matt's been flattering appears on the pavement before us, lighting a roll-up with one of her band mates. Her hair is the mirror image of Scott's; jet-black backcombed and pulled aloft. Moreover, she has red eye-shadow swaddled in circles around her peepers. Its shock-rock vogue, designed to make the model look like a sleep deprived zombie; the kind of slap Marilyn Manson was wearing ten years ago, inspired by Alice Cooper, several decades before that. Today it's homage to Gerard Way, frontman of new(ish) American emo sensations, My Chemical Romance. I'm increasingly aware that everybody here is turning into a miniature version of him; a sycophantic army of punk rock statuettes.

The other half of the tour party have been plodding around the town, attempting to amuse themselves with sex shops and petty theft. We reconvene on the pavement where John originally dropped us. Dan is tipsy; he's been drinking all the while. He jabbers with a thick French accent into a polystyrene shoe horn he's stolen from out of a display trainer in JB Sports. Lyndon is laughing at him. 'You should have seen him over there,' he says, breathlessly, pointing back at the town centre. 'There was a woman pushing a pram down the street and Dan went right up to her, right up to the baby inside it, and poked it in the head.'

'Eet was a doll,' Dan says. He shrugs, his shoulders slow

115

with drunkenness. 'I jus' wanna see why she's pooshing a doll.'

'What did she do?' Beth says. Her eyes are wide, her voice disbelieving.

'Nothing,' Gavin says, snorting. 'She walked away. It was a doll.'

I peer quickly at the digital clock on my mobile phone. It's four o'clock and there are still six hours until show time.

'Can we go to the pub now?' I ask.

White Dog Shit

The bar in Toby's Tavern is spacious and almost empty. The football results echo out of a television set fixed close to the ceiling. The carpet seems to be made from some kind of rubber, like a giant darts mat. The barmaid smiles broadly at me when I leave to carry the drinks back to the table. Gavin and Dan sit opposite me. The others have walked back to the tour bus. Sunlight from the dirty window reflects in the pint glasses. On account of his half-finished course of antibiotics, Gavin's drinking Coke. The slice of lemon hides beneath the surface as if it's ashamed of itself.

Alcohol is, for the most part, the drug between the 'sex' and the 'rock 'n' roll'. It's legal and therefore very easily obtainable. Bands are supplied as part of their payment with riders which inevitably include it, and then they play at an establishment licensed to sell it, to a crowd who are buying and guzzling it. This is the nature of the business. Throughout the eighties, the pages of rock magazines were filled with photographs of bands that spent all of their conscious time drinking. The images are embedded in my memory: Metallica with their cans of Budweiser, Tommy Lee and Nikki Sixx, cheeks brushed with cerise blusher, fingers clenched around the necks of whiskey bottles. Jack Daniels became an iconic product, the square bottle and black and white label instantly recognisable, as much a part of a rock star's image as a tattoo or a pair of leather lace-ups. When a fan got hold of Slash's 70cl bottle during Guns 'n' Roses' 1992 UK tour, reporting the content to be cold tea rather than sour mash, rock gossip columns went into overdrive; an indication of the acute importance of the link between rock music and booze – anyone who was anyone was a hard drinker, or at least they portrayed themselves that way.

I can't verify this behaviour, however, as an influence on my own consumption of the stuff. A working-class background already insured that I was adept at sneaking to the drinks cabinet to slug vodka neat from the bottle, whenever I felt adventurous; a direct result, probably, of my mother weaning me off my dummy by pacifying me with her sherry. During the Welsh coal boom, miners drank beer because the water was infected by cholera. Alcohol was a precaution that turned into a coping mechanism, something to deaden the pain, or enliven the workaday tedium. I learned pretty quickly that our type of life was supported by crutches and if the liquor-soaked lifestyle of my idols affected me at all, it was a quick wink in my direction, a confirmation that all was normal. My relationship with alcohol remains complicated. I've grown up to be a writer, a career in which the lines between intoxication and creativity can be blurred, and where I'm more often than not encouraged to drink like Dylan Thomas. There is a constant stream of material peddling through my mind, ideas for stories, words, names, memories, shopping lists... in effect, I am *constantly* working. The only way for me to interrupt this affliction is to drown it in a bucket of booze. But this temporary solution was handed down to me through the gene pool. My grandfather, my mother and one of my uncles were, or are still, alcohol dependent, and their fondness for it has not escaped me. I know for example that I am incapable of having one drink without having several others, and that Dan's pre-lunch can of lager was a precursor to having wound up at this pub. And tomorrow when I wake up, there'll be a kind of antsy itching in my veins, a yearning for a repeat performance; the hair of the dog syndrome. I have yet to yield to the urge but I know that the moment I do is the moment I become an alcoholic. A nine-day rock 'n' roll tour is the ultimate climate in which to test this theory. Time unfolds not in Gregorian calendar days but in moments, feelings, and places. To drive home after a gig and return to a new venue the following morning is simply a waste of fuel, but to drive from one venue to the next leaves big holes of time in the schedule and the obvious way to fill them is with alcohol. Sure, it's a practice best left alone because it leads to inadequacy, instability, addiction; finally death. Most music-related mishaps, overdoses, suicides and splits occur during long bouts on the road. And yet it's difficult to think in a sane fashion when you're stuck in an enclosed space with the same ten people for days on end, with nothing but condiment poker to entertain yourself. Alcohol is a constant temptation. At any given time you're either trying to recover from its effects or abstain from its pull, or you're submitting to it, hook, line. Sometimes, you're doing all three simultaneously.

In a bid to calculate his former record label's upcoming profit, Gavin is trying to multiply the festival entrance fee by the number of kids outside queuing, his hazel eyes staring hard at the table in concentration. The figure, he reckons, is something like ten grand. He sees the ink stamp on my wrist and asks if they made me pay. After a few minutes standing with Lyndon at the toll booth, haggling, they'd offered me entrance at half price: £3.50. 'Bastard rip-off merchants,' he says bitterly, cocking his head back towards the venue. He begins to tell me about the various forms of neglect he claimed Midasuno suffered. In the early stages of 2004, *When Bulls Play God* had cost money rather than earned it, the band members becoming suspicious, Midasuno had secured a support slot for Funeral for a Friend at a secret London gig. Scott asked them if their lawyer would look at Midasuno's contract, check it for discrepancies. A few days later when they faxed it, the lawyer annulled it free of charge. The deal was defunct by the end of the same day. Lockjaw Records, meanwhile, claim that in lieu of a mysterious batch of merchandise, Midasuno still owe them money. Now, one of Gavin's friend's bands has been offered a similar contract. He's told them not to sign it, and they think he's trying to discourage their success. 'The temptation of being in a signed band is just too much,' he says helplessly. 'In a few years time they'll be in the shit, but they'll only learn from their own mistakes.'

These kinds of mistakes are meant to happen, they're sent to try people, they sort the wheat from the chaff, they teach endurance, and I say so. 'A failed record contract here,' I say, 'a failed relationship there, it isn't really going to affect you.'

Gavin puts his glass on the table and sniffs doubtfully. 'Do you know what happened last night?' he says, lowering his voice, focusing his eyes on my own, 'with Scott and his ex-girlfriend? She only phoned him. Well, got somebody to phone him because she got taken to hospital, for being pissed, or something. She's never going to leave him alone. What can he do about it in Lincoln? It's emotional blackmail.' He's still staring at me as though he's expecting me to agree so I sit back and quickly consider the situation. I can see it from the ex-girlfriend's point of view; her partner disappearing to perform the musical equivalent of *The Full Monty* every night. I can see it from Scott's point of view: an ambition so driven, to refuse to follow it is to die. I can see it from Gavin's point of view: his frontman, his friend, is still being compromised by someone he's tried to leave behind. It's complicated. I nod glumly, but don't feel it's my place to comment. I sip my drink until his gaze withdraws.

Gavin's suspicious attitude towards me, concrete yesterday, has totally dissolved. He's speaking to me not as a journalist but as a friend, and I'm not quite sure how I should react. These little glitches appear occasionally in my conversations with Scott, pauses and sharp intakes of breath, as though he's momentarily wondering who he's talking to. For a reporter I'm exceptionally good at fading into the furniture. But Scott is media savvy and his words are designed for effect, he has a reputation to uphold and uphold it he always does. Back in Merthyr, when he told me that Gavin wanted to shag Beth, his comment was knowing, and deliberately spoken in my presence. Gavin's mention of Scott's ex-girlfriend, however, is genuine. It reflects real concern. If Scott is trying to create a sparkling representation of a rock band in their prime, then Gavin is trying to deny it. There's a friction in their relationship which may or may not arise from this difference, a sense that they're continually playing with one another; even when they're far apart.

I flash my cigarettes and Gavin takes one.

'I'm sorry the female company didn't turn out to be very stimulating,' he says. Chauvinistic men (many of whom can be found in the uneducated populace of the South Wales Valleys) do not expect women to think for themselves. They're often offended when they find one that does. Gavin seems shocked that he's managed to stumble upon one who doesn't. The jukebox starts up with a Coldplay track. Dan asks us if we hate the band. There's fierce opposition between mainstream guitar music, liberal in its approach, and therefore hugely popular, and 'real' rock music, the non-compromising likes of which have never seen the inside of a chart: majority v minority. He doesn't 'hate' them, Gavin says. Initially he liked one or two of their tracks. Then he saw the video to 'Yellow', in which lead-singer, Chris Martin 'prances' ineffectually along a beach, 'a silly, wet grin on his face'. It made him cringe. Dan says he's done their sound once, when they were starting out and Chris Martin stood for an hour chatting to him. Then he did it a few years later when Chris Martin had married Gwyneth Paltrow, and Chris Martin no longer recognised him.

Conversation meanders into uncertain territory, pub-going patter: Gavin's saying something about the nature of coincidence and how he half believes his life is a kind of *Truman Show*, beamed for entertainment on the televisions of the masses.

'It stands to reason,' he says, 'I bet my girlfriend's watching me right me now.' His notion seems a bit extreme but I agree anyway and tell him about my odd and reoccurring experience with the etymology of words: when I discover a new one, I check it in a dictionary, note its spelling and reference. Then, for some unfathomable reason, the following three days are packed with encounters of this very word; I hear it on the news, read it in a novel, the woman in a queue with me says it. What I want to know, and ultimately never will, is if the word has always been there, dormant and undetected, or if this occurrence is a complete coincidence.

'It's a bit like white dog shit,' Gavin says. 'You never see white dog shit anymore and I want to know where it's gone. I could ask you now why there's never any white dog shit around, and you'd say you didn't know, and then when we walked outside there'd be white dog shit on the pavement.' But I do know where the white dog shit has gone. Dogs don't eat bones anymore. They eat tinned dog food, Chappie and stuff. (I know, only because it's a subject my sister-in-law who works at a butcher's brings up regularly in house parties.) Gavin looks at me, the energy in the chatter evaporating. I've ruined his favourite topic of discussion.

'Okay,' he says, sighing, 'now I know.'

'Gav!' Scott shouts, bursting into the bar. He walks briskly towards our table and falls into a chair. 'I've found a girl who wants to fuck you!' There's a heavily pregnant pause while the information settles. 'So where is she?' Gavin says, smiling at me hesitantly. Scott disregards this gesture, adamantly slapping the surface of the table. 'Outside,' he says excitedly, 'she'll be here now.' The pub door creaks on cue. A daisy chain of blondes stream into the bar, bucking like turkeys. I watch them file past the cigarette vendor, average age sixteen, faces porcelain-like and empty. There's eight or so altogether. The girl we're waiting for is last, her eyes timidly darting about the room. When she spies Gavin she halts, pulling her hand free. Her mouth drops open and let's out a shrill and piercing scream which continues to resound even when she's run back out into the street, the door slammed behind her. Her friends shrug and sit down around Scott, hair twisted around their forefingers. Matt, who has

123

plodded in amidst the drama, sits down next to me. He picks
a beer mat up and rips it into quarters.

Girls, Girls, Girls

They sit with their phones set on the table before them, various colours, makes and models, but each containing a photograph of Scott with his arm around its owner. Some of these pictures, taken with my fumbling fingers, have already been converted to wallpaper. Scott smiles proudly out of the miniature screens, the digital clocks overwriting his forehead. It's Saturday 23rd July, 19.15. The band have left to unload their equipment, the sun turning small and amber-coloured. Dan and I are still drinking, surrounded by a gang of needy, female faces. Three of them are part of an all-girl rock group who play a cover of Midasuno's song, 'Tear'. Scott has told the lead singer, a short, plump, strawberry blonde, that she can join him on stage tonight for the chorus. She discusses the meaning of the lyrics, fingering the rows of pearls that land on her black cotton wife-beater. Scott is from the Patti Smith 'cut and paste' school of lyric arrangement. He writes a poem and then disembowels it;

stuffing the jumbled lines into the music, as though purposely confusing the listener. It's not always easy to interpret them in their new form but I'd been confident up until this point that it had something to do with sadism – 'choking back on polythene' – and gender politics: 'Oestrogen onslaught will rule against.' For some reason, she thinks it's about anal sex. She tells me the tagline I've been hearing for three years as 'She said she'd take my hand and put it somewhere else', is a misinterpretation. He isn't singing 'hand' at all. He's singing 'head'. I think about her argument for a moment. There's been much quippish talk amongst the boys about anal sex; mumbles meant to pass over mine and Beth's heads, as though as a different sex, we communicate on a different wavelength. Also there's a Biro drawing on the tour bus table of a woman balanced naked on all fours, the words 'up your guts' above an arrow pointing towards her. I realise though that this is moderately childish and inoffensive. Talk of anal sex is everywhere in pop culture. It's the new taboo – plain old vaginal doesn't cut the mustard in terms of shock tactics anymore; even Bruce Springsteen's got a song about it. But this arcane mention of 'head' and putting it somewhere else is all she has to support her opinion. I think if Scott were to broach the topic in a professional manner, he'd find a far more evocative way of going around it. Therefore, it's likely this girl wants 'Tear' to be about anal sex because it somehow satisfies one of her own issues. But of course it could be me who's wrong. Arguments like this are probably the stuff of Scott's dreams. It's evidence that he has a listener base, moved to try to construe his work. By delivering it in such an abstract manner he is able to attract differing opinions, insuring these discussions continue.

There's a blatant danger, however, in the ambiguity of songwriting. The most famous (and famously unfortunate) case was that of Charles Manson. He obviously did not know that the 'Helter Skelter' the Beatles were talking about was a slide in a British amusement park. He understood it as a call to himself to begin what was his idea of a revolution. As Sam Shepard, on tour with Bob Dylan, observed:

> Fans are more dangerous than a man with a weapon because they're after something invisible. Some imagined 'something'. At least with a gun you know what you're getting.

To glance at this girl, roses in her rounded and healthy cheeks, you'd never guess she had a care for anal sex, or anything else, even mildly obscene. It is the secret, highly emotive parts of us where the relationship between the adorer and the adored begins. The fan immediately believes, because a chord has so palpably been struck, that the artist knows them tremendously well, and that they in turn know the artist in the same way, as if there's a kind of telepathy between kindred spirits occurring. It's frenetic stuff. Dan, who has been watching our debate with great interest, suddenly takes his shoe-horn out of his combat trousers and answers it.

'Oh,' he says, passing it to the girl. 'Eets for you.'

Outside, the crowd has dispersed. It's between daytime and night. People have temporarily disappeared; home to change clothes and eat dinner. Just a few kids dawdle along the pavement holding polystyrene trays of chips, the vinegar stench permeating the street. Black Betty is parked on the kerb beside the entrance, the door open. What remains of Dan's

127

crate of lager sits on the front steps, the cardboard ripped. The record company have dismantled their stall. There are fairy-lights, barely visible against the daylight, thrown into the branches of the sycamore trees on the forecourt. Matt sits alone against the railings, drumming his thighs. He's pouting, he tells me, because his father didn't get back in time to lend him the money for the Misfits shoelaces. I release the ring pull on a can and sit down to sympathise with him, when a thirteen-year-old girl cuts across the pavement, followed by what look like two of her younger brothers. They're dressed in brand-name tracksuits and look conspicuous against the denim and the key-chains. That's why I notice them. She's about to pass when she sees Matt. She turns around and walks towards him.

'Man, are you fat?' she says, spitting on the tarmac between us. She stares for a few seconds and makes off, the little boys behind her laughing. Matt is silent, as though he's long since given up wasting energy on such comments. I want to say something to counter-balance this impertinent girl's rudeness but I'm not sure *how* exactly. It's true for one thing. He's fat, morbidly obese; nineteen stone or so. And yet he's not as fat as he used to be. The local hospital has put him on a diet of water and nutrients. In the mornings when we wake, John asks him if he'd like a milkshake or a chocolate bar, fumbling in a plastic bag beside his pedals. Matt consumes his breakfast quietly and for the rest of the day, eats nothing. How long this regime is going to last, nobody actually knows. To date he's lost four stone. His drumming has got much faster.

I take my phone out of my bag to answer an incoming text message. It's from Emily, my English lecturer friend. 'Hey rock chick,' it says. She's not a fan of the band, not particularly, not yet anyway, but she finds the fact I'm travelling around with them on their bus utterly compelling. 'How's the tour going?' At this very moment, she's in a wedding reception at the Heritage Park Hotel, two tables away from my fiancé. He looks lost without me, she says. 'I'm pissed,' I type haphazardly, the apostrophe in the wrong place, 'somewhere in England.' By the time I've completed this laborious task, Scott has reappeared, a can of lager in his hand. He's drunk too, I can tell. Alcohol turns his usually genial demeanour into a passive-aggressive disposition. He ceases to be interested in anything unrelated to him or his prime concerns, and his prime concerns are magnified. It's the perfect opportunity to get him to divulge fundamental information.

I ask him why the band is called what it is. Thus far I've dodged the question because it's a hackneyed line of enquiry which band members get bored of answering. That said a band's name is its most singularly important aspect, its point of call, its address to everyone who's not in it. The word(s) will remain with the band members for their entire life span regardless of their level of success and anything less than distinctive is bound to become a burden. Midasuno is an invented word I've learned to accept, having encountered it so often. (My-das-oo-no; it's easy.) And yet since I've embarked on this project, I'm aware that many people outside of the music community are unable or are reluctant to pronounce it, perhaps because there's an unexplained mystery within it, a feature which tends to raise people's defences. It seems to mean nothing but it must mean *something*. It's only a word but it could be the very one separating the band from a record contract. Do I want the truth, Scott asks, or a story? Both. The story is that Midasuno is an appropriation of a Welsh word that was given to a malevolent spirit that haunted the forest at the rear of Castle Coch. Matt interrupts this fairytale thread, seemingly uncomfortable with it. 'Tell her the truth,' he says. The truth, less strange than fiction in this case and much more tiresome, is that Matt liked the word 'Midas' and Scott liked 'Uno', a Muse song. 'But why Midas?' I ask. It's the name of a king whose touch turned everything to gold. Greek mythology is rarely cited in the big bad world of rock music and MIDAS, the Missile Defence Alarm System acronym, only became part of the English language in the mid-nineties, in keeping with the supposed threat of world terrorism. 'It's a character from a Playstation game I had,' Matt says, '*Tomb Raider*.'

Two girls are walking by when one of them stops and asks Scott if she can hug him. He holds her affably for a minute, the girl rubbing her face into his shoulder, like a cat trying to leave its scent.

'It's great isn't it?' he says when she's walked ahead, 'I can't pull in Merthyr but...' His sentence trails off and he thinks of something else. 'A big part of rock 'n' roll,' he says, 'is the mystery behind it. It isn't just about music. It's about sex and drugs, about wondering what's going on in the dressing room. When you go to a gig there's a security guard holding the backstage door but if he turns his back, there you are, you've got the golden ticket...' His voice halts again as more fans trickle past. The street is buzzing for a second time. I wonder for a moment why he's gone to the trouble of explaining this to me; surely it's obvious. But then I realise it isn't, not completely. I'm still stung by my last tour bus experience. At the end of 2003 when The Darkness were preparing for a gig at Cardiff University, I pressed my face against the blacked out windows of their bus, looking as I am now for evidence of the band members' superhuman powers, for their ability to live life on the edge and still be brilliant tomorrow; the unqualified glamour. What I expected were half-finished crates of Dom Perignon, the bottles upturned in silver ice buckets. What I saw was a ketchup bottle standing on its head, breadcrumbs littering a cheap, plastic chopping board; the debris of a peripatetic existence.

This is a poem from Henry Rollins' book, *One from Nothing*, written on the road with his band Black Flag in 1987:

In New Jersey she said:
'It's always been a dream of mine to have you inside me'
In Rhode Island six people came and no one clapped
In Pittsburgh she said:
'You're the most gorgeous man I've ever seen'
In Minneapolis the pigs arrested Joe
In Des Moines she said:
'It's so exciting when you come inside me'

It continues through another twenty-two US cities in its attempt to destroy this legend of life on the road by presenting his experience of it as humdrum. It's deliberately sculpted to appear repetitive and boring, but somehow never does. How can a teenager who stacks shelves for a living, who is probably itching to lose his virginity, find strings of groupies tedious? Scott, unaware of its momentousness, has just slipped me the ultimate truth, which is that a large degree of anonymity between the audience and the band is crucial. If fans somehow got to discover that their idols were as mortal as their low down selves, what would be the point in buying tickets to watch them? When a mystery is solved, the case is dropped. If the mystery, however, is never solved, the case always continues. It never really matters how many journalists step in, trying to demystify this process. We know that there are fabrications at work but for the most part we like to believe them and sometimes when you look too closely at something your own eyesight can damage it. It's like the Midas touch in reverse. This too is the nature of the business.

Lyndon is embarking on his daily excursion to the off licence. I walk with him, Beth and Chris in tow. We stagger away from the busy street, across an intersection into the eastern outskirts of the town, the wide pavements littered with chip papers. The band have become a dysfunctional but tight-knit travelling family in the way all co-working troupes eventually do, and Lyndon and Chris seem like its children; lanky wide-eyed men-boys still enchanted by their circumstance. Lyndon studied music production with Dan and Scott at Glamorgan University, while Gavin read English Lit. (He left halfway through his second year, Lyndon says. 'I don't know why. I read the essays he was doing and they looked okay to me.') But Lyndon, like Scott and Dan, has a degree; an accomplishment that seems to surprise him, perhaps because he still works his part-time waiting job at Brewster's. This means he's the same age as most of the other band members, twenty-two or thereabouts, a fact which I forget, partly because of his boyish appearance. Chris is younger, a nineteen-year-old who is deadly ambitious but whose collection of band-name T-shirts and belt buckles, and fixation with maintaining perfectly poker Johnny Ramone-style hair, seem on first impression as important as anything else. Age, I've noticed, is something I'm slightly obsessed by. Yesterday I realised I was the only member of the tour party to grimace when we hauled our luggage out of the hold and into the lounge in search of clean underwear. It isn't by any means a painful chore but the wrinkled brow is a habit I've picked up in the company of older people. My brother, my fiancé, most of my friends; they're a decade ahead of me. I've made a conscious effort to drop the scowl. My vocabulary too has suddenly slimmed. It's all part of an attempt to convince myself I'm young enough to be considered a contemporary of these boys, rather than a mother figure; a shallow insecurity which probably boils down to sex.

At the off licence, an Oddbin's whose strip-lights flicker on against the emerging dusk, Lyndon buys Casini, an even cheaper version of Lambrini. Chris gets a bottle of Jack Daniels. I'm waiting at the counter to pay for my six-pack and I've been here some time when I realise that the cashier is simply staring at me, smiling. 'What's wrong?' I say.

'I don't want to embarrass you,' she whispers, 'but I don't think you're old enough to buy these.' I glance over at the others who are waiting for me inside the door, all smooth freckled skin and giggles. 'I'm almost thirty,' I say, offering her my credit card. The cashier thinks about it for a moment, mutely consulting her colleague. Finally, she accepts it. I carry my stash back to the kids, pretending to be insulted.

Back at the Arts Centre, Black Betty has broken down. The boys are pushing her, their T-shirts riding up the small of their backs. They're halfway around the block when John manages to fire the engine. The starter motor is temperamental and he'll need to keep her running if we want to leave Worcester tonight. He parks her in her original space, sitting wearily at the wheel. I'm sitting at the table, listening to the iPod, watching the street through the blacked out windows. We're surrounded again by hordes of teenage girls. Tens of them have appeared from nowhere, little women in jean skirts and patterned tights, their faces besmeared with excessive make-up; lamb dressed as mutton. They skulk on the street, gradually getting closer like a circus of empty-headed and hungry zombies, the scent of flesh in their nostrils. Eventually, one particularly attractive fourteen-year-old is brave enough to climb the entrance steps. 'Can I have a look?' she says, running her hand over the upholstery. Her fifteen friends follow her onto the bus. Some of them take pens out of their handbags and sign the table top, avoiding eye contact with me. Chris is lying on his bunk, the bottle of Jack Daniels tilted in the air above his face, his skinny legs crossed. When they see him they step into the bedroom and sit on the empty beds admiring him. They don't speak English these girls, they simply purr, like elegant, predatory animals. Despite his taste for grown-up whiskey he appears young, friendly and almost asexual so it's reasonable that the teenage girls flock towards him but he enjoys his monogamous relationship with his Welsh girlfriend. 'I pull them,' he says, 'so everyone else can fuck them,' proud that his appeal is of use to the rest of the band.

One of the most interesting stories in Mötley Crüe's confessional, *The Dirt*, is Nikki Sixx's account of a party at their shared house near the Whiskey A Go-Go in Los Angeles. He was having sex with a drunken groupie in a wardrobe when he suddenly got an idea to go outside and call Tommy Lee into the wardrobe and let him have sex with the groupie while she still believed the man penetrating her was Nikki. When this was successful he went back out into the party and found another man. He too had sex with the groupie. All the while, the word on her lips was Nikki; 'Oh, Nikki, Nikki.' I suppose it's difficult to see a woman you don't know particularly well as anything other than a sex object when she's all but begging for it. Nikki Sixx was woken the following morning by a telephone call from the groupie. She told him she got raped last night. 'I was hitchhiking home,' she said 'and this guy raped me in his car.' Where the moral of this story lies, I'm not exactly sure. The rock scene, by its own admission, is a rainbow of various shades of grey.

Chris ignores the girls however, his lips clamped around the neck of the bottle. It may be because they're exceptionally young (the youngest here is eleven), or it may be because I'm recording it, or it may be because that's what he usually does. The band's general talk of past experiences with zealous groupies is for the most part bravado. Midasuno, for the moment at least, are a hundred miles away from the notorious party antics of Mötley Crüe. Indeed, they're more perturbed than thrilled by this invasion. Scott bursts into the sleeping compartment and packs his belongings into the cupboard under his bunk where prying hands can't reach them. John orders the girls out of the bus, shooing them hesitantly like snappy terriers. Beth and I have to prevent them from returning while the boys change into their suits. We stand on the entrance steps, blocking the gangway, while Gavin crouches behind us, quickly binding his tie. The fourteen-year-old turns puppy dog, smiling imploringly as she sidles slowly back towards us. I'm reprovingly waving her away and somewhat enjoying it, when I get a text reply from Emily. 'Fab-u-jealous,' she says.

Forget diamonds. Nothing attracts a woman like a tatty, old, and broken down tour bus.

It's Down to Us to Start the Riot

The auditorium is crammed. Kids stand on the dance floor, staring. Rows and rows and rows of them, all locked together in a purely intoxicating miasma of fire-breathing noise, like particles being sucked into a highly strung vacuum cleaner. The people on stage have ceased for a moment to be the people I know. They're something else now, a tight group of hypnotists capable of short-circuiting kid's brains; contortionists who writhe like boa constrictors in a bag, instruments throbbing. Scott grinds his teeth and slaps himself in the head. A boy in the front row cups his mouth, mesmerised by it. His girlfriend wipes her eyes, smearing mascara across her cheekbone.

I'm sitting stage side, propped up against a giant pillar. Every few minutes, I hiccup, the contraction in my throat making me jolt. They're inaudible next to the music, but I can feel them, and short of asking a stranger to plug my ear canals while I hold my nostrils closed and swallow a slug of lager (an old cure of my Nanna's), there's nothing I can do. Dan and Beth are in the second row, bobbing in and out of view, the half-empty bottle of whiskey passing occasionally through their fists. At the end of a song, Dan passes it to Scott and he gulps it fitfully, the thick base obscuring the lower half of his face. The strawberry blonde materialises, her eyes frozen in terror. Scott puts his arm around her shoulder, forcing her towards the microphone, the crowd screaming encouragement. This audience loves this band. This band loves this audience. There's a cloud of rapture drifting throughout the room.

When they launch into 'Start the Riot', a tight little foot tapper, the opener on *When Bulls Play God*, something extraordinary happens. I suddenly forget all that I've learned about the band over the past two days and revert back into a fan. It's something to do with the lyrics of the opening verse:

> I can try harder than the last time.
> Sharp, bleak as fuck. This is our SOS.
> Gagged, caged by narrow minds.
> Decide. An instant of pain.
> Not enough, you complain.
> I know that I can try harder than the last time.

It could mean anything, anything at all, and yet I interpret it as an anti-Thatcher stance. I see for a moment, exactly what I want to; five kids from a post-industrial wasteland with no real meaning left in their lives; the children of socialists who have been put out to pasture and who are really fucking angry about it; people who are just like me. Sure, they don't look like they care much about politics and they're singing this supposedly Marxist anthem to a flock of kids who look like the only revolt they're capable of starting is a skirmish with a McDonald's

138

employee about their Big Mac not coming with Super Size fries, but as a fan I need the band to make me feel less alone, to be people who have experienced the same thing as I have and speak my words when my voice can't be heard. 'It's down to us to start the riot,' Scott sings, and the crowd shouts, 'it's down to us to start the riot,' back at him. The riot I'm thinking about is the Merthyr one of 1831 when radical workers rioted for five days until they were massacred by British soldiers. That's why the first line of the chorus says, 'I can try harder than the last time.' These men are my champions, the people who are going to stand up and say 'Screw capitalism, it means nothing'. The other people in the crowd are probably thinking of some other riot, a riot of their own, but any sort of riot is good, anything that's passionate, anything that's rebellious. We sing the chorus as one, our forefingers thrust at the ceiling. It's a superb proclamation of solidarity, the culmination of all our body heat swimming in rivulets down the pillar beside me, goose pimples marring my arms. The hall is an oven, baking up a mixture of noise and sweat; a big messy mutinous youth pie. My nerve endings are like candle wicks, my adrenaline is dynamite; anyone comes near me with a naked flame and I swear I'm going to fucking explode.

At the end of the set there's an eruption of applause. Scott stands soaking in it, contemplating his next move. He hasn't finished yet. I spot a potentially volatile situation in the wicked smile playing on his mouth; the audience stood solemnly waiting on him. Fortunately, seemingly content with the performance, he only pulls the light shade above him from its socket, balancing it comically on his head.

The hall is still half-full when Beth comes over, her once neat ponytail ruffled. She's trying to pull me up, and saying

139

something I can't understand, her lips dancing quickly, when I notice the altercation on the stage. Ben and another man who looks a lot like Ben are standing behind the sound desk, shouting. Swearing and pointing at Scott like school teachers in the midst of nervous breakdowns. Scott stands insolently before them, their words hitting him and bouncing off. The remainder of the band are swiftly packing their gear, their faces twisted with a mixture of laughter and alarm. Leads coiled in record time. I concentrate on the argument in an attempt to deduce its origin, the crowd still filing around me. The light shade is the problem. It's the property of Worcester Council and Lockjaw Records have taken it upon themselves to protect it with their entire wrath. I stand listening until the quarrel is over. The boys have gone outside and the light shade sits innocently in the position in which it was left. Beth holds my wrist, trying to tug me towards the exit. I wave her away. I'm driven instead to approach Ben and his friend. This may be because I understand Midasuno's plight. God knows I've had my fair share of inept literary agents. Or it may simply be because my favourite pastime after more than a couple of drinks is troublemaking. In any case I tap one of them on the shoulder presumptuously, and offer to fix the light shade. For a while this is a playful exchange; me insisting that it's not damaged, them insisting that it is. I think it includes a few 'How many music promoters does it take to fix a light bulb?' jokes. Then I hiccup and one of the men laughs at me. I launch into a barrage of insults. 'How amateur you are,' I say, 'to allow such an incredible band to perform such an incredible set then berate them over something as trivial as a light shade.' Uglier words than that, but working towards the same effect. Ben looks blankly at me, pumping his decorated arms. 'And they don't scare me either,' I say.

When I retreat, Dan arrives. He confronts them with what I initially assume is French. After a while I realise it's gibberish. He stands between them, his hand pressed adamantly on his hip, utter bollocks rolling off his tongue.

Gavin is carrying an amplifier across the forecourt. He says we have to get the gear out of here, as quickly as we can. Spurred by adrenaline (and the scene in *Almost Famous* where Stillwater escape an irate promoter by driving through a locked gate), I pick an amplifier up and follow him, the weight twisting my torso. When award-winning photo-journalists who document famines and wars are asked why they never become involved with their subjects, why they don't feed the starving, why they don't seek aid for the wounded, they say it's because they're professional, because their job is simply to record. That's bullshit. Human beings are foremost human beings, and here's where the journalist turns into a person. Here's where the telling gets jumbled up with the being.

'Fucking hell, Rach,' Gavin says, squinting disbelievingly over his shoulder. 'I didn't mean you.'

'It's heavy,' I say, limping.

'Yeah, 'course it is,' he says, giggling, the fairy lights in the trees reflecting in his pupils. Then he stops giggling and simply smiles, the ginger stubble on his chin two days old. Time slows to a stop. There are people around us moving, walking back and forth, but they're blurs of colour in the corner of my eye, their outlines indecipherable. We stand in the middle of all this action, totally still, totally smiling, for a second, two seconds; I don't know how long it is. Then normality begins again. Gavin drops his amplifier and goes back to the venue for another.

141

At the bus the pandemonium continues. Ben has followed Scott out to resume their squabble, and is leaving again, clenching his fists, swearing to himself. I catch the tail end of the sentence which is 'throttle the little cunt'. Scott, oblivious to this, is leaning against the door jamb of the gear lock-up, surrounded by equipment. 'Do you think I used the right hand?' he's saying as he digs the air with his pointed finger. 'I used my left hand. Perhaps I'd look better if I used my right, more imposing like.' He switches hands, comparing their effects. 'What do you think?'

There is a gang of girls lined up against the railings. One group is watching proceedings very closely. I can see them through the hinge of the door, waiting for something. John asks me to look after the bus and ventures into the building in an attempt to resolve the issue. As he passes they ask what the problem is. 'Bad blood,' he mutters impatiently.

'Backstage,' Matt says, looking at Scott, 'Ben said you're not as big a rock star as you like to think you are.' I glance at Matt's face, trying to work out what this comment means exactly. He's the only member of the band who's stone cold sober. Is he trying to rile him further, or make a valid point? The words are loaded but his intentions are vague.

'ROCK STAR?' Scott says, his long black hair stuck to his head with sweat. His eyes jump out of his face, half crazy, half blank. He looks dangerous. 'Rock star? It's better to want to be a rock star than to *be* a fucking Mongol. Ben's a fucking dick who never went to school. He can't read.'

Lyndon arrives with more equipment. The girls call him over. He waves, but drops the stuff at our feet and runs back to the venue. 'Anyway,' Scott says, 'at least I told him to fuck off. You hardly ever get a chance to tell someone to fuck off.

142

Fuck off. Someone you always have to be nice to. Fuck off. Fuck off. I told him. Fuck off. FUCK. OFF. FUCK. OFF.' In an attempt to break Scott's chain of cuss words, I tell him that I too told Ben to fuck off. Scott stands looking at me, amazed, either by my interruption to his speech or my choice to involve myself in the band's troubles. I'm not sure which but he gulps a mouthful of air, as though he's about to start ranting again. Then he swallows it, breathes again and makes off to talk to a fan he recognises.

Suddenly Dan comes swaying out of the gate and stumbles into the group of girls who are watching us. They scream. He growls at them, baring his teeth like a psychiatric patient doing an impression of a black bear. He rolls around on the floor in front of their feet.

Half an hour later the bus is branching onto an A road, the lights of a garage lonely against the open fields, three or four miles away from the Arts Centre. Lockjaw is going to send the bill on when they've deducted the cost of the damage. Gavin's got hold of some cannabis and he's smoking it at the table. Everyone's calming down, the spat only worthy now of reminiscent smiles. I'm sitting in the gangway in the bedroom, scouring my hold-all pockets for a new packet of cigarettes, when Scott steps abruptly through the curtain, his arms flailing. He's staring at me wildly. 'Come on sweetheart,' he says, tapping his mattress. 'You need to go to bed. You need to borrow my bunk again.' He starts shifting clothes around, throwing them onto the spare beds. I stand aside watching him. I don't actually want to go to bed, but I do want to borrow his bunk again. He whips the corner of the sleeping bag back and points at it. 'C'mon sweetheart, lie down.' I sit on the bed. I can hear 'Prick of the Day' start up around the

143

table and I want to go and play. Beth nominates Chris. 'I lent you my hair-straightener, didn't I?' Chris says, affronted. Scott nudges me softly and I fall into bed, my head hitting the pillow. He kneels down beside me, attempting to fasten the sleeping bag. It's a white sleeping bag with brown piping and brown cubes printed on the exterior. The day after the near orgy incident with Frankie, I laid in it for twelve hours, the gratis house vodka gradually sweating out of my pores. My mother-in-law washed it especially. I begged her not to. God knows what sort of stains its going to come back with, I said, Darran frowning worriedly at me. Now the wash cycle has stiffened the zip. The pull is caught on its jagged teeth. Scott's head is an inch away from mine. 'It's sticky,' I say.

'It is sticky!' He says, yanking it valiantly. 'C'mon you cunt,' he says, whispering at it under his breath. The snag releases and he fastens it to my chin.

Dan starts growling again, his low voice vibrating across the moving floor.

'Okay now?' Scott says. 'You're okay now.' He pats my elevated feet as he climbs back into the bus. 'Dan, you wanker,' he shouts, his voice getting faint as he closes the bedroom curtains behind him. 'Stop being so bloody passionate. You are my prick of the day for being so bloody passionate.'

One of those girls has Tippexed her telephone number on the ceiling above me; the digits thick and white. I can still smell the noxious substance. They twist on the slats, dancing like animatronics until they vanish. The screen goes coal, coal black. The riot's over.

Good London/Bad London

It's drizzling as we set off for the capital. 'Wet rain', our parents call it. Thin rivulets stream out of the snow-white sky and drip down the windows. They tap on the sun roof, becoming heavier as we hit the motorway. I woke this morning to news of Scott having tried to 'mount' me in the night. Lyndon says he was sleeping on the top bunk, one leg hanging out of the mattress and swinging like a stuffed doll's, when he rolled out of the bed and fell like a cadaver to the floor. Everyone else, still talking stoned talk around the table, was alerted by the crash. Scott stumbled up and shot them the evils before trying to muscle into his own bed, me already inside it; wrestling with the sleeping bag for close to ten minutes before settling for Gavin's empty bunk opposite. I hadn't felt a thing, I said, although Scott should have realised I was there. He put me there. 'Alcohol!' he says, shaking his head repentantly, his make-up smudged on the sheet. It's too early for innuendo, Matt says, sitting up. He lifts his arm, jiggling his fingertips against Scott's: 'Morning,' Midasuno style.

There's also a new face on the bus. Ryan Day, guitarist of Aberdare band Pete's Sake, and good friend of Midasuno's, joined us at some point after last night's gig. Pete's Sake had supported Midasuno on the first leg of the tour but there are rumours afoot that they're about to split up: a few of their members have mortgages to pay and life on the road has become a hindrance. Ryan had rung Matt's mobile phone two days ago, saying he wasn't going to make it; he was due to sign on at the benefits counter on Monday. Matt told him to conjure an imaginary funeral, for an imaginary relative. Even job-seekers had rights when it came to bereavement. (Matt, apparently, has done this many times.) He's a short and pleasant boy with long, curling eyelashes and a smile that ripples across his whole face. He has a large P tattooed on the back of his left arm, and an S on the back of his right. After his breakfast joint he collects all the pot-smoking paraphernalia; the papers, the lighter and the pot itself, hiding it behind the blank destination banner for fear of a chance police spot check. The tour routine has etched itself into the interior of the bus. Shoes, clothing, motoring maps, magazines, liquor-stained gig-contracts, books, empty bottles and food cartons compete for space. No one is bothered this morning about cleaning any of it up.

Last night's frivolity has worn to a dull hangover. We sit around the table picking sleep-glue from our red and swollen eyelids. Music, the great unifier, has been forfeited; all sockets occupied by phone chargers. Silently, we devour a stack of Sunday tabloids, somebody laughing or sighing occasionally at a story about a celebrity. It's a fortnight since four suicide bombers boarded three tube trains and a London bus, and blew themselves up, killing fifty-two innocent commuters besides. Exactly one week later, four new suicide bombers attempted to copy the attacks, failed, and then escaped. When I left the house on Friday, Sky News was reporting the assassination of a suspect at a London station, gunned down by undercover detectives. Yesterday's cover stories, which I saw fleetingly in a service station, claimed the man was innocent. Offenders have yet to be caught; some victims have yet to be treated. Security in the city is on high alert and the newspapers are still full of it. Nobody mentions this until we're close to Richmond and a fleet of riot vans buzz past us, sirens wailing. The motorway lanes are lined with Greek and Indian kebab houses, their shutters pulled down against the dim Sunday light, the dome roofs of mosques holding a distant skyline. Ryan thrusts the centre pages of the *Mirror* between my crossword and my eye-line.

'Do you know London?' he asks. 'Are we going anywhere near this?' It's a diagram of the areas affected by the bombs, the tube stations flanked by a death count and a roll of cartoon flame. I look at it for a moment. All of the terrorist activity seems to have been centred on the circle line. We're going north.

'It's fine,' I say, passing the paper back to him, the pages shuffling. Matt says worrying about terrorism is pointless. He believes in fate: when your time is up, your time is up. Everyone agrees.

It's sometimes a long way from one's world to *the* world and life in the South Wales Valleys is no exception. For the most part, it's a particularly grim and isolated place from which to come. Surviving one giro day to the next is a struggle. Events that only affect other people are often beyond imagination. I heard Gavin at one point, for instance, ask Scott if the country we were at war with was Egypt. It was a joke of course but its humour was based on a very real sense of apathy. I remember visiting New York for the first time, aged twenty-three. An all expenses paid reading tour, organised as part of a talent exposure initiative in October 2001. Before the event, in September, aeroplanes hijacked by terrorists destroyed the Twin Towers; the British Council offered a get-out clause and many of the other artists took it. I didn't, and I didn't think for a second about doing so. My lifelong ambition of setting foot on Times Square was at stake. And set foot on Times Square I did, the financial district still billowing yellow smoke behind me. I was waiting on the sidewalk outside the hotel for a taxi to Carnegie Hall later that week, when Richard Evans, a fellow Rhondda author, approached me. Pointing at the entrance to Madison Square Garden opposite us, he said, 'How mad is this? Two kids from Treorchy on the middle of Seventh Avenue!' I was trying at the time to convince myself of my cosmopolitism. New York City is the gargantuan airport of Planet Earth, its crevices packed with human beings of every possible nationality. Just standing on its sidewalks encourages you to think of yourself as urbane. But to be able to understand Richard's utter disbelief, I had to be a Valley girl; no messing. The thought of being in London, and not in Merthyr, kindergarten compared to New York though it is, seems to be enough of a topic to fill the boys' heads. I glance under the flyover at the entrance to Edgware Road tube station, the ginger-tiled façade specked with rain water. Scott notices it too. 'That was one of the stations, wasn't it?' he asks, gravely. There's quiet for a moment, and then it's gone. Black cabs gather around us and a flurry of arms reach for their newly-charged mobiles, an overture of key-tones sound as Midasuno's London contacts receive text message invitations to the show.

My own experiences with London have been strange and somewhat varied. On a Tuesday lunchtime in November 2003, I was with Darran in the middle of Belsize Park, looking at a fern tree perched on a doorstep, its leaves turning rusty in the wind. Busy people who work in the media don't have time to look after their plants. I was thinking about stealing it, but we had already parked illegally, in a residents' only bay, sitting in my step-father's BMW estate, which we'd borrowed because our own car had broken down. It didn't occur to me to knock the door. It was Rosie Boycott's after all; first female editor of a national broadsheet and regular panellist on BBC *Newsnight Review*. What would I say? Hello Rosie, I'm Rachel? She'd nominated me as the UK's most promising young writer for a *Harpers & Queen* magazine feature in which influential people in the arts were to be photographed with their chosen protégées. The photo-shoot was in her living room. I feel funny describing it – even thinking about it now, it seems positively surreal. When the photographer and his assistants arrived, along with the deputy editor, the make-up artist and my agent (who'd unnerved me insufferably by pointing flippantly at a white stone three-storey a block away and saying, 'That's where Madonna lives') we gathered on the porch like a group of carol singers. Forty-five minutes we stood there, the freelance make-up girl clutching the handle of her giant pink vanity case, as though willing herself back to *Smash Hits*. My agent, my latest manuscript packed in a manila envelope under her arm, was peering into the bay window. 'No, nobody here,' she said, 'she's got a wonderful Flokati though, here, take a look.' Fittingly, Boycott had stood me up. But the madness did not end there. Apparently, Martin Amis, as well as Madge, lived in the same area. If we asked him nicely, he might stand in. At the risk of appearing difficult, I shook my head, murmuring something akin to 'no'. The photographer, an enthusiastic upstart from Shoreditch, began banging on about an original set, something which didn't involve books. I took this opportunity to mention music. I wanted to sit at the bar of the Electric Ballroom, a cocktail in one hand, a cigarette in the other, men in bondage trousers milling around me. Camden, however, was out. A gang of skinheads had mugged the deputy editor there when he was sixteen.

Come five o'clock we were driving through central London, heading for a cramped Stoke Newington bookshop, where Peter Florence, director of the Hay literary festival, was going to meet us. The make-up girl and the deputy editor were sitting in the back. I watched him through the wing mirror check the Rolex on his wrist. I was wondering what the benefit clerk at Treorchy job centre would make of all this. Only twenty-six hours earlier I'd sat in front of her, my jobseeker's record full of faked entries. 'Have you thought about learning a new skill?' she'd said. With that question in mind the photographer's jeep halted at a traffic light, Darran clipping his bumper. We ignored the existence of this little mishap, like a fart in the company of mere acquaintances. It was six o'clock when the make-up girl looked out over the sea of rush hour traffic. 'This thick white smoke,' she said, 'seems to be coming from our bonnet.' The deputy editor ran to Spar and came back with three bottles of Evian. He poured them in the overheating radiator. Later, he'd have an argument with Peter Florence about the reputation of his Italian tailor, while Darran dealt with the RAC. We were driving past Battersea Power Station that night, showers of luminous green fire-work shards exploding against the black sky, when my step-father's name flicked across my phone screen.

I still see Rosie Boycott on the TV, untouchable as ever (except now I know where she lives). My encounters with her city have gradually worked themselves into a three-faced equilibrium; good London/bad London/plain old bizarre London. I get a feeling for its mood as I arrive. Today though, there's just no telling.

Scott slaps Beth's shoulder and asks how much money she has. Camden is a veritable curiosity shop. There's bound to be something there she'll want. Her slick, black hair is fanned across the table. She lifts her head, yawning, and it falls back into place. 'I've got a hundred and sixty quid,' she says. 'My mother gave it to me. She packed my bags too. Is that enough?'

'Your mother packed your bags for you?' Matt asks dubiously.

Chris emits a sharp snarl. 'What sort of mother...' he says, and then promptly thinks better of it. He looks down at the graffiti he's been working on; a boy with a stomach full of cars, based on Scott's earlier fluff. (He'd pointed out of the window, meaning to say, 'Look at that car full of boys.') The words hit the world, breached. John pulls up suddenly at a bus stop on the High Street, the bus bucking backwards.

Gay for Johnny Depp

The buildings here echo with good memories. I glance around and breathe them in: the HSBC bank where at 18, late for an interview at St Martin's College, I queued for the cash machine behind an MTV presenter. Later, I'd highlight the withdrawal on my bank statement as evidence of having been somewhere so cool. The Dickensian World's End pub where I sat for a whole day with my mate Station, drinking cocktails and wasting pound coins on the novelty of a steel tipping tray. The cracked pavement in front of the tube station where having earlier signed a Curtis Brown contract I hopped around elatedly, Darran squeezing my hand like a proud Dad. Camden is a massive Bohemian souk that beckons suburban sub-culture-orientated youngsters from around the country, like moths to merchandise heaven. It's where they buy their green hair-dye, their cats-eyes contact lenses, their glow in the dark tattoos, their PVC nurses uniforms, their eyeball piercings and swastika iron-on patches. Then they take the train home, rifling impatiently through their purchases, anticipating the horrified looks on the faces of their neighbours.

It's probably the only place in Britain where Scott, clothed in his black suit and cerise eye-shadow, looks ordinary. He leads us along the pavement in an invisible anorak, his jowls highlighted only by his acne, his shades nowhere to be seen. I raise my hood against the drizzle. We eat chicken curry from polystyrene trays. It's been a couple of days since I've eaten anything warm. I can feel the chunks of meat coursing through my oesophagus like fire.

The boys flick indolently through monochrome prints of Johnny Depp, framed in a poster turnstile on the corner of a street. They've been talking throughout the tour about going to watch *Charlie & the Chocolate Factory* when it's released on Wednesday. Apparently, the Oompah Loompah men have been digitally augmented; something which should only be witnessed under the influence of very strong hallucinogens. Admiration for this particular Hollywood actor is intense at the fringes of society, including the rock music community, based in no small part on his eclectic choice of roles. He played Hunter S Thompson in an adaptation of *Fear and Loathing in Las Vegas* and a cocaine baron in *Blow,* and even based his character in *The Pirates of the Caribbean* on the Rolling Stones guitarist, Keith Richards. Recently I saw *The Brave*, in which Depp stars as well as making his directing debut. It's the story of a Native American man who sells himself to a snuff movie director in order to feed his impoverished family. After doing so, he's paid half of the fee and given a week to enjoy it before submitting to his torture and murder. Johnny Depp is great. We all think so. There's even a new all-male rock band called 'Gay for Johnny

Depp'. We move on to an indoor bazaar where Beth buys a belt buckle and a cigarette case. I'm flicking through Tori Amos vinyl when Matt finds a red and black striped skinny tie, the word 'cocaine' embroidered with white cotton along the shaft. He suggests the whole band gets one, each with a different drug. 'Baggsy not heroin,' Chris says, thinking about the implications. 'Baggsy heroin,' Scott says, thinking even harder.

Back on the street, we're huddled in a doorway dodging the rain, when a wide-boy shuffles by. 'Hash-hish,' he whispers. 'Hash-hish, hash-hish.' He glances quickly at our faces, ensuring his message is received before retreating into the crowd of shoppers. We watch him vanish. Stand still long enough in this area of London and you'll get offered drugs you've yet to hear of.

Drugs are supposed to be the lifeblood of rock music but throughout the tour there have only been many anecdotes about them. Scott has talked in length about his experiences of acid, one form of drug I've always avoided. Hallucinogens are mind altering – a factor which scares the living daylights out of me, and presumably always has. Aged five I found my brother's magic mushrooms wrapped in newspaper at the back of the fridge and emptied them into the kitchen bin. There's also been talk of class A stimulants. 'Was I on coke?' Scott asked, while Matt reminisced about a Saturday night out in Cardiff Metro's. Not least there have been many mentions of poppers. Its real name is amyl nitrate; a noxious liquid added to diesel in order to improve ignition quality. Inhaled, it's used to heighten sexual pleasure, or provide a short physical buzz followed by a ticking headache. The trend at comprehensive school was to tip a quantity on our ties to snort later in boring geography lessons. It seems to be totally harmless. There are

155

crates of the stuff stacked in the shops around us, retailing at approximately £4 per 10ml bottle. But no one is attempting to purchase it. With the exception of marijuana, a legal narcotic (providing you suffer from multiple sclerosis), nobody from Midasuno has ingested drugs in my presence. I did of course consider the implications of bringing drugs with me, as I had alcohol, but realised it was literary entrapment. Drugs, like drink, only seem to be an issue while they're present. Users, Midasuno may be; abusers I'm certain they're not.

The band split up to pursue their individual interests. Gavin and Matt go looking for tattoo parlours. Lyndon buys postcards. The afternoon sun beats on my back as I walk with Scott towards the venue, the rain puddles drying up. On our way we approach a fairly anonymous boutique, the walls of the flat above it painted black and flanked by ornamental dragonflies. The shop is called Dragonfly. 'It's Nikki Sixx's,' Scott says. I peer incredulously at it. Nikki Sixx's experience of London was a heroin overdose in a Hammersmith terrace where the dealer then dumped his dying body in a plastic wheelie-bin. Of course, he woke up a few hours later and went out and scored again. Inside the shop, the rails are sparsely occupied by customised rock T-shirts; Misfits and AC/DC wife-beaters embellished with glitter and rhinestones. Mötley Crüe has become a prominent feature of the entire tour; their music playing perpetually in the background. I remember on the first day, cracking a bottle of Corona open while the motorbike intro to *Girls, Girls, Girls* blasted out of the iPod. At the point where Vince Neil shouts, 'Hey, Tommy, check that out, man,' and wolf-whistles, suggesting the sight of an attractive female strutting along a sidewalk, Gavin was doing the actions, his arms around his band-mates' shoulders, his finger pointing into the middle distance. I decide to buy a T-shirt. When the cashier is packing it for me, I find myself wanting to ask her if her boss, Nikki Sixx, ever pops in. Having seen past some of the myths of one rock band, I've begun to buy into those of another.

I'm sitting at the table reading, while the band load into the Barfly. Ryan is standing in the doorway of the bus smoking a reefer, blowing his fumes out into Chalk Farm. 'Is your project for college?' he asks. I tell him I'm almost thirty and that a woman in Worcester asked me for my ID last night. 'So she should,' John says. 'You don't look a day over sixteen.' That's his conversation opener. He goes on to ask my thoughts on Lockjaw's approach to the light-shade, 'the palaver,' he calls it; trying to work out which side I've taken. 'Oh they were very unprofessional,' I say, frowning. It's early in the evening and Along Came Man have pulled up facing us in a hired transit van. The telephone number sign-written on the wheel arch has a Rhondda Valley dial code. 'He's gonna be sorry leaving that there,' John says, 'its arse end is sticking out.' Their girlfriends pull up in a separate car with a couple of friends in tow. One of them is Chris's girlfriend. When they see each other they cuddle in the fire exit, their faces obscured by a mixture of their straight black and curly red hair.

Beth is outside, sitting on the stone doorstep of the locked pub, the sun obscured by the high-rises towards the west. There are still three hours until doors open. I ask her if she'd like to go for a coffee and we walk back to an Italian cafeteria in Camden Town. She skims the froth off her cappuccino and sucks it from the bowl of her stainless steel teaspoon, staring at the cake display beneath the counter. The satsuma segment pushed into the cream topping of a chocolate sponge has dried up under the artificial light. I compliment her on her lip piercing and tell her about my tongue. Actually informing someone that there's a hunk of metal speared through one of my vital organs is a rarity. A lot of the people I meet have seen it already in the publicity shot on the back of my novel. They point at my mouth and ask if it's still there and I poke it out and they smile and that's the end of it. I'm unnerved when she says, 'It's nice, and it could be useful for *something*.' It's that reference to lesbianism again.

My youthful riot girl experimentation with homosexuality is almost ten years over. I'd go gay for Wendy James if she still looked like she did in 1991, and Kate Moss at a push, but I'm straight and wholly convinced of it. What I'm slightly concerned about is how female bisexuality has become a kind of fashion item worn purely to titillate men, like a mini-skirt or a pair of stilettos. Of course she could mean it's a useful tool for giving blow-jobs, in which case she'd need to consult Darran. Something in my face must reveal my discomfort because she apologises and tells me about the book she's reading; a women's short story anthology. Because books have changed the course of my life, undoubtedly for the better, I have an idealistic notion that they'll do the same thing for everyone else. I'm sure now that she's not the kind of teenager who'll get pregnant and move into a council house. Anyone who can read a book can organise some contraception. Anyone who can read a book can teach themselves to aim high.

It's another balmy night; the blacked out windows absorbing the last of the day's sun. The air in the living room is humid. Black Betty's engine is still purring. The boys are getting ready, dressing slowly between cans of lager. Matt stands in the road at the side of the bus, chatting mildly to an early arriving punter, a girl he met at a previous London gig.

He tells her about his phobia of feet. I understand now suddenly why he stares and winces at mine. I love feet; especially my own, and I bare them wherever possible. He also picked one of my flip-flops up out of the gangway earlier and threw it at Beth's head. 'Clean your shit up, will you?' he said, blushing when I took it from her and slid it on.

The girl asks about the progress of the current album. It's the end of July and they're still recording. The venture began in October 2004; more than nine months ago – the process lengthened unbearably by full-time jobs, A Level examinations and a plain lack of funds. It's already swallowed a thousand pounds; money straight from the band members' pockets. I get the feeling their producer, Nick Lloyd, a man who commands a quarter of that figure per day, regards them as a labour of love. It's almost finished, Matt says; maybe Christmas. They need to put the orchestra down. It's not a real orchestra, obviously, but by all accounts it sounds like one. The frustration in his voice is almost tangible. All the members talk constantly about it. It's the best stuff they've ever made. They're bursting to release it, and completion is so, so near. So near, and yet so far. On the subject of money, Lyndon tells me I could make some by auctioning my book dedication on eBay. They go for hundreds, he says. But dedications are meant to be heartfelt – a sincere address to a respected mentor. Some of the boys turn and look at me sympathetically, as though this is a feeble point to make; toughened as they are by this starving music school of hard-knocks.

Dan sits on the floor beside me, worrying. His girlfriend was rushed to The Heath hospital during the afternoon when, whilst cooking dinner, she collapsed for no obvious reason. He told me earlier that the head engineer he has to work with tonight recently launched a hate campaign against him, publishing a letter in the *Barfly* industry magazine accusing him of incompetence. This detail is insignificant now. He waits for news of a diagnosis before accepting John's offer of a cancellation. Scott is standing in front of the Hyper Value mirror, an eye-pencil in his hand. John boards the bus proclaiming the presence of two very important reviewers; one from *Rock Sound*, the other from *Kerrang!* Scott shoots him a vexed look, his finger still holding his lower eyelid down; the pink flesh beneath his eyeball exposed. 'Thanks a fucking lot, John. That's exactly what I wanted to fucking hear.' Ryan steps out of the bedroom and lifts a bottle of deodorant out of the wreckage. He sprays it up his T-shirt, asking, somewhat belatedly, who it belongs to. Scott snatches it keenly and squints at the small print concernedly. 'Don't just pick things up like that, Ry,' he says. 'Somebody could have injected it with a poisonous substance.' I look at his face for a glimmer of a wry smile. There isn't one; he's serious. These regular fits of paranoia are a little troublesome. The first time I met him he told me his local authority were spiking the tap water with excessive fluoride in an attempt to keep the population of the Valleys stupid. Behind him, Beth sits with a new pair of tights splayed over the table, struggling to cut their feet off with the edge of her door key.

The Art of Self-Delusion

The doorwoman is settling into her shift, smiling agreeably from her wooden toll booth. She holds a white clipboard close to her chest and I make the mistake of trying to look at what's written on it. Getting in on a guest list is an art form, whether your name is down or not. I know it is because I saw Scott write it. Do you know what my surname is? I asked, interrupting him. 'Yeah,' he barked. 'And I've fucking spelt it right.' But I've been turned away from my own literature readings before now, once for not looking like a writer. Give a little power to someone with a menial job and order goes tits up. She snatches the clipboard closer to herself, seemingly hurt by this gesture, and holds it in place with one arm, awkwardly ink stamping my wrist.

The stairs leading to the venue are covered in black linoleum with glittery silver flecks sprinkled in it. Every step is marked with a glob of chewed and discarded white gum, or a squashed cigarette butt. The indentations of heels push through the linoleum revealing the light wood underneath. Five minutes ago I was standing in the Chalk Farm street, talking to Darran while two fat pigeons bathed in a rain puddle beside me, and now as I climb the stairs, the trapped noise in the auditorium getting closer, I replay our conversation. Neither of us said anything out of the ordinary. We talked in clipped sentences, calling one another 'love' as if to emphasise the status of our relationship without actually touching on romance. This is how we always talk. But once, a few days after 11th September 2001, he rang me from work saying that the people in those burning buildings had been people who went to work one day, and simply never returned. 'Know that I love you,' he said, 'in case one day is today,' and I feel for some reason I can't immediately fathom, that I should have reciprocated that sentiment this evening. Only three days into the tour, I'm already tired of it.

The concert hall is smaller than my living room and almost empty. Along Came Man have just completed their set; the frontman Andrew says something about the band having their debut video played on rock music channel, Scuzz. There's some tinny applause from the girlfriends who have gathered at the far end of the bar. Beth stands with Matt's friend beside two German students. John and Ryan are hanging T-shirts up next to the entrance and a man in a pair of green combat cut-offs, who may or may not be a reviewer, kneels on the floor beside the stage. I order a ladylike vodka and lemonade and walk to the front, overwhelmed by the space around me. Midasuno go on and launch into 'Shock Horror', their current breakneck opener. Scott calls it his 'call to arms to a generation desensitized by entertainment'. It's about incest. They spread their legs in their black trouser-suits, their heads shaking rhythmically.

Immediately, my mood lifts, negativity instantly purged, and I begin to wonder why this is, why rock music always excites me, always saves me from whatever I'd been worried about only minutes before. During a question and answer session at a literary festival in 2002, the interviewer asked the Italian novelist Marco Mancassola, with whom I was sharing the stage, why so many young people were becoming novelists. Mancassola said that he really wanted to be a rock star, but that he couldn't be, so he wrote books instead. I found myself nodding, unaware until that point that I really wanted to be a rock star. Despite my early efforts to perform, music didn't have the urgency of literature. Creative writing was so immediate, I often fool myself into believing it chose me, not the other way around. I thought about it for a few months, deducing that I was an artist concerned primarily with communicating. How the communication manifested itself, in words or notes or pictures, was less important. I was only jealous of rock stars because they got triple the amount of attention for a quarter the amount of work. But if my prose had a sound, it would be the urgent crash of rock music.

This is why I'm spellbound by Midasuno. They're a compound of everything which has influenced me in some way, the LA glam scene of the late eighties with all its leopard skin and indulgence, the New York punk scene of the late seventies with all its spittle and chutzpah, Trent Reznor's dark and brooding industrial neurosis, the debauched and disturbed writing of Hunter S Thompson and the dogged pop rock of the Wildhearts. Not to mention the fury of having grown up on a council estate in the poorest part of Wales, a thousand miles away from where all this good shit happens. They say more about me than any other band to emerge from the country, which is why I think it's

163

crucial they get signed. Of course there are ingredients in all Welsh pop music, in all music, which appeal to me; the basic map-plotting lyrics of the Stereophonics, the melancholy of the Manic Street Preachers and even intermittently the gloss of the Lostprophets, but there is something lacking in all of these bands' approaches to their origins. The Manics wallow in their Welshness like misery. The Lostprophets appear to deny it. Funeral for a Friend play on it. Midasuno do nothing more than accept it. Council estate Merthyr, 'the rhythm machine', as Scott describes it in a song of that title, is the place which made this band what it is – a conglomeration of good influences and proper hungers; wallowing in thoughts of Valley oppressiveness and delighting in ambitions of escaping it. Standing here watching them blend place and personality together so seamlessly, I feel like a narcissist in a mirror, and for forty minutes every night they make the impossible seem possible – they turn being Welsh and desperate into something akin to sexy.

All this, given that Midasuno are an unsigned band, may be a little presumptuous. I never quite know how to introduce them because while they are regarded on an underground level as one of Wales' best bands, the mainstream remains oblivious to their existence. They don't sell platinum; at the moment, they don't sell anything at all. But Scott has always been sure that the band would 'make it.'

> The graveyard of bands that *nearly* made it is massive but we're not going to end up there. (April 2003)

> ...we will be embraced by the British rock public and be able to make a living out of what I really love doing. (April 2004)

164

We're either going to come out on top or we are going to die doing this. There is no middle ground with this ride, this rocket we're on; it's going to go right up or it's going to come crashing down and there will be bits of us everywhere. (July 2005)

I'm inclined to believe him. At times his self-belief is nauseous, bordering in fact on self-delusion. There is an art to this and Scott has mastered it. The most important thing one must understand when facing a laborious obstacle, i.e. getting famous, is that conviction begets conviction. When you believe in yourself, even against all odds, it's likely that others will too. I've forgotten how many times I made claims of being a published author before my debut novel was even complete. I was an arrogant little cow the whole time, but given a bit of talent and a lot of determination, my gamble paid off. Whether Midasuno's will is entirely another matter. The music business is a tough and extremely competitive one, prone to chewing dreams up; an attic full of freaks with a trap door that beckons you closer, only to slam it in your face. There seem to be two ways into its hall of rock fame. Either you're an original and unique talent who spends an age honing your skills until eventually it cannot ignore you, or you're a band who sound like some other band and you get lumped in as part of a pocket-lining music 'scene'. Are Midasuno an elephant, or the mouse that sneaks in on its back? I'd like to think they're the former and that all they have to do now is be in the right part of the river when the A&R hook goes fishing. But how long exactly will that take? New bands, like premiership footballers, have a short shelf life. In this milk and honey city of cities, with its huge population of artist and repertoire

165

people, nobody has turned out to see the band. I'm getting frustrated for them.

Beth comes to stand next to me, a plastic tumbler of whiskey and coke squeezed between her fingers. She rises up on the toes of her pumps and cups her hand around her mouth. 'They're not as good as yesterday,' she says. I spin round to acknowledge her and, from the corner of my eye, spy Chris shouting the backing vocals to 'Start the Riot' into his microphone, the parts the audience are meant to shout, his eyes staring out of his dark fringe. Here he usually raises his arms and claps hands above his head, encouraging the audience to join in. But there is no audience. This song is a lonely venture, given yesterday's unruly delivery. The band aren't playing any less well than then, except it's difficult, I imagine, to interact with a wide open space. What's clear suddenly is that some of this band's allure stems from their determination to be successful rather than their actual success. It's fairly easy to party after all. To build something where once there was nothing is a more taxing endeavour. It's the bricks at the bottom of the pyramid that hold the ones at the top in place; the bands who go out and tour the country knowing that they might not get paid enough to cover the petrol home and nevertheless persist, where taking the rough with the smooth is par for the course: that's where real heroes are shaped. Midasuno play this gig to nobody, their heads held high, and I am more impressed with them than ever.

Back on the bus, the mood is sombre. Ryan tucks silently into his Subway sandwich while Gavin sucks languorously on a joint, the smoke swelling grey against the artificial amber light. When my head is turned he smirks and directs it at my hair, believing me to be oblivious. Scott is sitting in the gangway folding the strewn clothes into a neat pile; the socks paired and balanced on its surface. 'What's my favourite Midasuno song?' I say, asking them to hazard a guess. After a roll call of their back catalogue, Matt gets it: 'Hypocrite'. It's the last song on *When Bulls Play God*, a mellifluent, brooding little number in which Scott repeatedly calls his love interest 'a fucking hypocrite'; bitter-sweet to the core. Gavin sucks air over his teeth and tells me it's a hard song to play live. I didn't ask him to play it live.

Double-Yolk Mother-Fuckers

The shower only dispenses water while the stainless steel knob sticking out of the grubby beige tiles is pressed in. The shampoo sachet from the vending machine cannot be torn open with my wet hands. I bring it to my mouth and bore a hole in the foil with the tip of my incisor, the detergent splattering out onto my tongue; metallic tasting and sharp. It reminds me of disinfectant-drenched childhood swimming lessons at Ystrad Sports Centre, the girls lined up against the walls in their bathing suits, their arms folded rigidly at their waists. My milk white skin never matched up to their holiday tans. Showering was a matter of shivering beneath a sprinkler only long enough to wash the verruca treatment out of my toes, and running into the changing room in time to get a cubicle with a curtain. Even now when I take my nephew to the same pool, I can smell the insecurity of my early teens.

I'm frantically trying to scrunch my hair dry in front of the water-stained mirror (it takes two hours with the aid of a hairdryer), when another woman comes into the shower room; a tall, blonde twenty-something with a peach complexion.

'Sorry,' she says, standing next to me. 'I have to be in work in half an hour and I've only just left a house party.' She takes a concealer stick out of her handbag and runs it around various parts of her face, like war paint, before manically blending it in. She's almost finished when she notices me again through the mirror. I ask her where she works, assuming she's going to say *here*, in the service station, because for four days that is the only formal work I've seen anybody do – pour drinks and fleetingly, serve food. 'A bank,' she says. I nod sympathetically, having forgotten temporarily that it's half past eight on Monday morning in the real world. 'Will you look at my eyes?' she says, widening them as she turns to me. Her pupils are so dilated it's impossible to distinguish the colour of her irises. Whatever stimulant she dropped, it's still fully functioning. I think it's wearing off, I tell her.

Back at the bus I sit on the gearbox and pass one of two cappuccinos I bought at the overpriced breakfast cart to John, my pockets full of sugar sachets. The police knocked on the door last night, he says, wanting to know what we were up to, before they retreated to the other side of the car park and bent to look with their handheld mirrors at the belly of a rusty Vauxhall Cavalier. Unfathomably, he links this occurrence to religious fanaticism, telling me that they should put undercover officers in mosques to record what's being preached. He toys a two pound coin out of his trousers, saying something about Enoch Powell, when I cough, deliberately interrupting him. I look past him, through his window, at the swollen clouds moving quickly above the service station, their middles white, their edges slate-grey. John smiles apologetically, leaning into my eye-line. Do we have a house, me and my boyfriend, he asks, and what does my boyfriend do? I tell him he's a welder. John's been a welder, and a freelance bodyguard. Men of his generation, who come from the South Wales Valleys, always seem to have lived wildly interesting lives. The despoliation of the area during the Thatcher era seems to have made them all incredibly enterprising. You still hear rumours in the workingmen's clubs, in the Rhondda at least, about the one who single-handedly robbed a TV warehouse, leaving only one reconditioned portable behind, or the one who married an aging French millionairess. And yet they always seem to end up in the autumn of their lives, their adventures hidden behind their mottled skin; back on the sick, apparently racist, and living through the ambitions of their children. Opposite us, the three members of Along Came Man get out of their Transit van with water pistols, the van doors thudding. They play war games on the forecourt. 'You must have seen some things,' I say, almost subconsciously. He's been driving the band about since it began. Most of their fans know him by name. All of the girls know him by name.

'On the road with this lot?' John says, 'Yeah, five years we've been doing this now. They've played with some bands. I don't know how they cope when a band that used to support them gets signed, Funeral for a Friend and that.' He cocks his head at the bassist of Along Came Man as he stalks across the forecourt, the barrel of his brightly coloured plastic gun tucked under his elbow.

'But John!' Scott says. 'Those bands are using powdered milk and shit. We're organic, free-range, double-yolk mother-fuckers.'

I smile to myself. 'That's a quote, Scott,' I say, prising the curtain back to look at him. 'Yeah,' he says, yawning, 'write it down.' He flops back into his sleeping bag, wrapping his arms around Gavin who's next to him. Gavin moans contentedly, nudging his head into the crook of Scott's shoulder; like lovers grasping for a flicker of intimacy before the alarm bell sounds and the world severs them again. A few weeks later I'd see an HTV programme in which the co-presenter Nicola Heywood-Thomas said Troedyrhiw was the best place in Wales to go vox-popping. I'd think back to that comment, cocksure and dashing.

Tonight's gig is at the Satan's Hollow in Manchester, a venue which Midasuno have yet to play. 'It's wicked,' Ryan says, eagerly. 'The stage is a raised circle in the middle of the room. The kids can watch from any angle they want.' We're sitting on the entrance steps, smoking, while Matt tidies the bus, waiting for the others to come back from the shower, when John's mobile telephone rings. It's the promoter cancelling the show. The club owner has closed up for a week and flown to Italy to tend to a family death. Matt wants to forge ahead, onto Sheffield in preparation for Tuesday's gig. John shakes his head. We already have Wednesday off; Glasgow cancelled as it was at the beginning of the tour. The light shade incident in Worcester has left us short. Without tonight's payment we don't have the cost of fuel to get us to Sheffield and even if we managed to scrape it together the amount left over would not feed and entertain us. A day off does not provide a rider; it's more of a burden than a luxury. The bus is silent while we slowly do the maths in our heads. The boys have to get back to Wales, raid their parents' refrigerators, and start afresh in the morning. One by one the others arrive, rejuvenated, and turn miserable when they hear the news.

The journey home is stolid. For the most part nobody

hoists their faces out of yesterday's papers. Dan is sitting next to me and I count from the corner of my eye the number of times he reads a tabloid story about the second round of London bombs. He doesn't bother to turn the page over but repeatedly returns to the opening paragraph. Three hours slip away. There's one moment of humour when Beth floods a service station carpet with hot chocolate. She's standing in front of the vending machine with a paper cup underneath the boiler when the liquid starts overflowing. When the drain is full it runs down the base. Beth is simply staring at the instructions. 'To stop press button once.' She's looking for the button which has 'once' printed on it. Gavin laughs contemptuously at her. I tell him a story about a girl I know, who, when confronted with the advertising slogan 'Buy a pair of Levi's and win return tickets to the US', said, 'Return tickets aren't much use are they? How would I get there?' He doesn't seem to find this nearly as funny. Lyndon pulls the iPod from its shelf and asks us to create a collective playlist; three songs each. Gavin starts with Meat Loaf, the dashboard confessional, in which the teenage girl, about to put out, asks the teenage boy to vow to love her forever. Of course he does, and twenty years later he's praying for the end of time to hurry up and arrive, because if he's got to spend another minute with her, he doesn't think that he can ever survive. Everyone knows the song, and I'm happily singing the female vocal when Matt looks scornfully over at our side of the table and says, 'What the fuck is this? It's awful. What is it, some kind of rock opera?'

John drops Chris off in his native Tredegar. We continue travelling. We pass a Merthyr Tydfil road sign, the words 'is shit' messily spray-painted next to it. Lyndon points at it and the

173

other boys nod submissively. It's not graffiti but a given, unspoken truth. Matt irritably requests a piss stop on Dowlais top. He says he's been asking since way back in Monmouth, the driver continually ignoring him. Now he can't wait any longer. Ryan stands and looks out of the window, the mountains surrounding us carpeted in yellow grass. The sky promises rain.

'I need a joint,' he says opening the miniature trap door behind the destination banner. There are no cigarette papers left in the orange Rizla cartridge so he drops to his hands and knees, searching for a plastic pop bottle – anything he can turn quickly into a bong. While he's down there he puts his nose against the gearbox, like a dog who's whiffed the scent of a treat. 'Something's burning,' he says.

The gearbox is dead. The bus won't move. Gavin rises gallantly out of his seat and swaggers to the dashboard. 'I'll have to sort this out,' he says, squinting at me. He prods the gearbox cover a few times. When it's clear he can't fix it, he loses interest and scouts around the floor for an empty bottle again. John tells Matt to ring their band agent. The remaining three gigs of this leg of the tour have to be cancelled. They're not going to get the bus fixed, or find new transport by tomorrow.

'We're Midasuno!' Matt says. 'We don't cancel gigs.'

'You have to cancel these gigs because there's no way you can get to them.'

'Fuck,' Matt says. 'You can't tell us what to do. You're not in the band. You're nothing.'

'I'm the tour manager,' John says.

'Yeah so?' Matt says. 'You're not in the band.'

'I'm the tour manager,' John says. 'We haven't got a bus. How are we going to get to Sheffield tomorrow?'

The rest of the band is sitting around the collapsible table, staring out at the horizon, their lips clenched shut. A drop of rain hits the window and Scott focuses on it, his forehead pressed to the glass. He puts his forefinger against it and follows its path as it slowly dribbles down. I climb out of my seat and walk towards the exit, my mobile telephone in my hand. I'm going to arrange my transport home. 'Fuck,' Matt says again as I pass him. 'See?' John says, catching my eye. 'See how he talks to his father?' It's the exact phrase my friends' parents used to say at junior school, an attempt to embarrass their kids into respecting them. I glance back at the scene from the doorway; the band turning from baby rock stars back into young men, men with jobs and girlfriends and fathers, right in front of my eyes. Luckily, Darran is in Pontypridd B&Q, buying something for his garage. He can be on Dowlais in ten minutes. I leave Midasuno on the mountaintop waiting for their own lifts, the yellow grass blades behind them, bowing in the wind. Betty, fat and useless, shows no perceptible remorse.

That night, I'm lying in bed watching the news with a giant bar of chocolate in my lap, when footage of the aid crisis in Niger shows a starving child, grappling for its dying mother's nipple. The chocolate turns hard in my mouth. I spit it into my hand, knowing as I do, that the tour bus bubble just burst.

PART THREE

Paper Stone Scissors

It's Thursday 11th August, 4.55pm in a Wetherspoons to the east of the city, the patio area flanked by Devon's signature palm trees. Curry Club starts in five minutes. The boys are sitting with their support band, The Next Nine Years, on a raised No Smoking lounge, their five pound notes on the table, and the menu cards in their mitts. Sunshine pours through the plate glass windows behind them, illuminating their ragged clothes and pallid skin. They're three-quarters of their way through the third leg of the Midsummer Murder Tour, despondent with hangovers. 'Fancy seeing you here,' Scott says, hugging me.

Almost three weeks have passed since I saw them last, fraught and cheerless; stranded like Brontë characters on a cruel and blustery moor. In Midasuno terms, fifteen days is a long time and the band has altered significantly. They've taken Ryan on as a sixth member. He's going to play guitar, leaving Scott free to handle the singing. They've already played

Compass Point, Wales' premier rock festival, under this guise. The official explanation is that Scott has damaged his hand. Photographs in the music press have shown him pink-eyed and pinstriped, his wrist hidden under a chopped up pair of women's black tights. Here, in a tatty red T-shirt, his forearms bare, the damage looks suspiciously like self-mutilation – a ladder of scabbing welts crawling towards his elbow. I glance down at my own long time scarred forearms. As healed as they're ever going to be, my skin looks like the stretched rubber of a ribbed condom. He's on his way out of the door, to buy a football in the Toys R Us superstore across the road. (They've bought a new one every day of tour only to lose or burst it.) Lyndon and Chris, still jubilant with last night's journey to Yeovil where they watched zombie thrash metal band Send More Paramedics, call me over to relate the event.

'The singer's about six foot two,' Chris says breathlessly, his brilliant eyes soaring out of his black fringe like marble. 'All the kids are there waiting for the band to start and he comes out of the toilet pushing them aside, marching to the stage, blood dripping out of his mouth.' By 'kids', Chris obviously means people who are older than him. It would be another two months before Midasuno would beat Send More Paramedics to the number one spot on the *Rock Sound* 'best track' voter poll.

It's nine years since I'd last been to Plymouth but the city still feels like a kind acquaintance. Earlier I walked the sun-kissed Hoe searching for the exact spot in which my photograph had been taken, sitting beside the Barbican with my crochet book bag, eighteen years old, my hair bleached blonde. The picture sat now on Darran's bedside table, its defective frame leg perpetually slipping away from it. It was taken on a holiday planned around a university interview at Falmouth

Art College. I was going to study journalism under a blue plaque declaring Virginia Woolf had done the very same thing, bridging gaps of generations by moving to the locale of my forefathers, and I would have, had I not failed my English A Level. When I stood in the Pop Factory telling Frankie I was part-Italian, it was a bare-faced lie, invented to make my bloodline sound alluring. Some people assume that Trezise is an Italian name and often I let them. The reality is personally much more intriguing. My father's ancestors were tin miners who split Cornwall to dig coal. Some went to America, the others to South Wales. My mother's great-great-grandmother was a Brittany gypsy who roved her way to West Wales, trading her teenage daughters as house maids to the crachach. To get all the way to me, there are quixotic anecdotes involving gentlemen abdicating their estates and marrying their servant girls, an old fashioned *Pretty Woman* plot; the fiction perhaps of my parents and theirs. What's clear is that I'm a 57 Variety Celt, made so by the discovery of the South Wales coalfield, and shaped at least in part by the south west.

At four o'clock I found the tour bus on the kerb outside the venue; as black as Betty but three times smaller. Iron Maiden's band logo was painted across its hip in white gloss, the words 'Europe – 1986' added at the end. The boys had draped a Welsh flag across the windows. John, as ever, was sitting in the driver's seat.

'I managed to borrow it,' he said, 'bloody tiny.' I looked inside, at the lack of space preventing my staying on it. Dan was sleeping on the floor, his hair fanned out around him. In the corner, an indoor barbecue – bits of age-old burnt meat were still clinging to the grill. 'So have you heard?' John says. 'They secured a support slot for The Misfits' Welsh gig next

181

month.' I had heard. Internet message boards were clogged with posts of disbelief. The Misfits are a phenomenon; a punk band's punk band, a household name, and one of Matt's favourites. There's only one original member left of course, Jerry Only (only by name, only by nature). It's as close to The Misfits as anybody's going to get in 2005; another name to drop on Midasuno's already glowing support slot CV.

Before the show we're standing on the Phoenix Street pavement, the boys changing their T-shirts and drinking their bottled Heineken. It's the student area of the city but it's the dead of summer and the students have gone home. Scott is perturbed by the lack of audience and he walks me to the side of the venue where there's a gig listing taped to the window. All of the bands are charted according to audience attendance.

'Last year we came top,' he says. Midasuno is the first band on the list with three stars printed beside their name. *'Energetic live band from Wales – highly recommended.'* I shrug. The absence of a crowd does not make Midasuno a less momentous band. They're even more noteworthy for being bothered. If a tree falls over in a forest and makes a loud crash, but there's nobody there to hear it, does it really make a loud crash? The answer is yes. I came to this conclusion on the last leg.

'Oh, boys!' Lyndon says, stepping out of the tour bus, a frown etched over his features. 'Have you ever tried to play stone/paper/scissors with yourself?' He bangs his fists against the air repeatedly and opens his hands into two sheets of paper, staring at them confusedly. 'It's really fucking hard.' He shakes his wrists again, trying to fool his brain into playing a game invented for two people. Within the minute, the rest of the band, along with the support band, is imitating him, unaware that the tour routine has numbed them even to their own thoughts.

The pub has one room, painted purple. The stage takes up half of it. I wonder if there was a crowd, where they'd fit exactly. As it is I can sit at a table and watch them comfortably. I'm their one and only punter. 'I forgot to tell you, Rach,' Scott says, talking into the microphone. 'I don't play guitar anymore.' Ryan, the man who does play guitar now, launches into the set list. Scott, far from not having anything to do with his hands, as is often the case when you take an instrument away from its player, shakes manically; crushing his hands into tight fists, like a baby unable to express itself yet with speech, on its first exhilarating Christmas morning, juddering his hips like a mentally ill version of Elvis. He's rolling his eyes into the back of his head, grinding his teeth and literally pulling tufts of his hair out. At the end of a song he thrusts his hand down the front of his jeans and tauntingly readjusts himself. Meanwhile, he hasn't missed a single word of the lyrics. Similarly, Ryan has learned all the Midasuno songs. Anyone who has ever tried to play guitar and sing at the same time will know that it isn't as easy as it often looks. It's solitary scissors/paper/stone territory. I'm aware suddenly of how distinctive Scott's voice is. Groups with more than five members for me always conjure images of fragile egos; twelve piece orchestras the frontman interviewed personally. I generally live my life against the *'If it ain't broke, don't fix it'* proverb. But the decision they've made, whatever its origin, does not diminish any aspect of the band. It's just another mouth to feed.

Gavin comes from the stage to my table.

'I'm pissed now,' he says, slumping against the back of the chair, as though this somehow explains why he hasn't spoken or even looked at me, at any point prior to this. As is now customary, we babble about body art. Without the consent of my brother, or even a glimpse at his increasingly

183

occupied appointment book, I offer Gavin a tattoo, free of charge. When the bar has closed and I still want one more drink, I ask Lyndon for a bottle from the rider. They're all gone so he storms bravely to the bar. I follow him. He speaks not to the bartender, but to John who is negotiating the band payment. 'Can you ask the staff for another bottle for Rachel?' I drink it, watching the band reload the gear. The side of the pub where Scott had shown me the gig itinerary is lined with prostitutes waiting for business. Elsewhere, the street is indigo-coloured and tranquil. I can hear some of the boys making muffled, echoing jokes about paying for sex in sixths; a little bit each, as I turn the corner on my way back to my B&B on the Hoe.

When I checked in yesterday the robust landlady was excited about the arrival of her mother. She opened a plastic grocery bag on the counter to show me the bottles of Scotch she'd bought her, pointing at the folded wheelchair in the foyer. But there's no sign of the landlady, or her mother. The dining room is empty, laid with claret-coloured tablecloths, the cruet sets, white porcelain. I manage three goblets of concentrated orange juice and one slice of buttered toast. It's been a restless night, wracked with nightmares about my own mother getting eaten by an alligator. My blue glass bottle of Kronenbourg 1664 still sits on the doorstep, hidden behind the railings, the pink lip-gloss print dried on the rim in the parching morning sun. I use it as an ashtray. Up on the Hoe beside the big black statue of Francis Drake playing bowls, a local radio station is erecting a temporary band stand for its annual pop concert, much to the curiosity of the local dog walkers. Charlotte Church is the headline act on Sunday. Today is Friday, the penultimate day of the Midsummer Murder Tour. Midasuno are already in Somerset, sleeping in a caravan and picnic park on the outskirts of Yeovil. The hotelier on duty, a tall, athletic man in his early fifties, asks me if I've enjoyed my holiday. I simply answer yes, save a long-winded explanation about being a journalist following a rock band on the road. What rock band? He'd ask, expecting me to say Bon Jovi or Deep Purple and getting disappointed when I didn't. I begin the four-hour drive to Somerset, a seemingly endless motorway trudge aggravated by iridescent sun glare and slothful tractors, my fingers buried in the bumf of the glove box in search of a foil card still swell with Nurofen caplets.

There's a free car park behind Yeovil's main shopping drag, surrounded on three sides by local authority offices. After a lonely franchise-style pub lunch, I park up and wait for show time. The vertical blind in one of the council windows has broken. Two of the beige slats hang out of the open porthole, blown around by the light wind. I wait for one of the workers to notice and come and haul it in, their face burdened with civic accountability. After a while I begin to imagine what's going on inside the office. I'm reminded of the job I gave up to implement this expedition; a temporary sales and purchase ledger in a local seatbelt factory. A den of politicking white collar snobs, so discontented with their own uselessness they'd turned their resentments onto the blue collar workforce in the factory below them, their court shoes pressed against the coarse carpet tiles, their whole lives moulded around inane bureaucracy. Working for someone else is permitted slavery. Friday afternoon is a miniature act of emancipation and tonight, thank God, it's them instead of me. At its most basic, the quest to become a celebrity – a rock star, a big-time writer or artist – is an escape route out of the domicile of the taskmaster. Very few artists are actually celebrated of course. Often the ability to express yourself without the burden of a boss asking you to do the photocopying every half an hour is a dream in itself. Come 5.30 I'm woken by a phone call from the *Rhondda Leader*; a work experience reporter wants to interview me about the launch of my new book, *Fresh Apples*. Local newspapers are the nemesis of good quality journalism. I answer the girl's artless questions, my mouth dry with sleep. When I look up at the council office the window is locked, the blind fixed and closed. I change, crouched behind the passenger seat from my white cotton wife-beater into my green and red polka dot camisole; the transition from pink bra to red, a modern feat of manoeuvre. One thing about not being on the tour bus is the ability to dress like a punter rather than a roadie. I slip into my beloved green leather heeled calf boots and make down to the venue.

Flicks is a small hall and nightclub situated on a one way system road at the entrance to the town. It's hidden behind another, larger nightclub which hosts a disco and a clientele a decade older. A group of security guards in black bomber jackets already stands guarding the disco. Across the road there's an executive log cabin cocktail bar called The Globetrotter. Its large screen televisions project silent coverage of the *Big Brother* final. The only thing which suggests Flicks is even there is its pink neon name tacked to the side of its crumbling brick wall. The boys are playing football on the forecourt of the adjacent tyre specialist garage, the tour bus parked on a nearby grass verge. The rhythm guitarist from the Next Nine Years, a healthy-looking almond-skinned blonde, has kicked the ball into the guttering at the lip of the roof and is climbing up the drainpipe to retrieve it. The rest of them are standing around directing him, Gavin with his trademark boxer-shorts blistering out above his blue jeans. Lyndon and John are at the steps of the tour bus discussing John's boyhood frolics. Time was he used to catch a train to Cardiff with his school mates and spend the entire journey climbing out of the half-and-half window, stalking across the top of the moving carriage and scrambling back in on the opposite side. Does Matt know about it? Lyndon asks. 'No way,' John says. 'I'm not allowed to talk about myself when Matt's around. He pulls a muscle if he sees me so much as speak to a woman who's not his mother; "You're a married man, you're a married man."' They stop chatting when they notice me. 'That's a nice top,' John says, in a manner which makes me want to button my jacket and hide it. The other boys wave, but continue their game. My heels prevent my involvement, although I used to play football in a men's five-a-side pub team. They stuck me in goal for the most part. I go to the club to relieve Ryan of his merchandise stall duties. The entire establishment seems to be run by eye-linered sixteen-year-olds. The doorman is a jumble sale table of teenagers erected on a foothill at the rear of the zinc construction, their pints of cider placed on the ground among the clumps of grass. The bar staff aren't old enough to drink what they're selling, the DJ too young to buy what he's playing. It's like a scene from some kind of punk rock *Bugsy Malone*.

It is however the scene of one of Midasuno's liveliest performances. I can see the kids crowding around the stage, afire with zeal and admiration, the backs of the guitars held high in the air to make room on the stage for the massive audience. The 'Start the Riot' lyrics come not from Chris and Scott but a multitude of adolescent voices. Even the kids who have not ventured to the front to watch them are startled by it. Couples stare mid-snog. A boy standing in front of me attempting some kind of bizarre mime artistry, his face painted clown white, halts and runs to the stage. It's a highly impressive spectacle worthy of my attention but I'm virtually asleep; sleeping with my eyes open, my hand cupped around my glass of lemonade in an attempt to deter drug rapists. I'm perfectly cream crackered. As soon as the show is over I go back to the car. Gavin is outside loading the drum cases into the bus, overjoyed with his performance. I think he forgets himself for a moment; he kisses me and bids me a good journey. On the garage forecourt there's a police car, the two policemen inside supervising a locksmith while he secures a window in the garage. There's a football-shaped smash-hole in the pane. Three hours later it's three o'clock in the morning and I'm turning off the M4 into Llantrisant. The Rhondda Valleys open up in front of me, basins of fluorescent orange fairy lights strung in zigzags across the low sapphire sky. Home; by night it's the most charming place on Earth. I have to pinch myself to confirm I'm not sleeping again when the darkness throws up a kid in a Misfits T-shirt, running from one side of the road to the other, inches away from my bumper, green Mohican and all.

Some Sort of Goth Band

The taxi driver has a tremendously infuriating habit of dismissing me as Darran's 'Mrs'. It's one of my pet hates. 'Like your Mrs is saying,' he says, glancing at Darran through the windscreen mirror, 'music is a matter of personal preference.' For God's sake, cut me some slack, I'm sitting in the cab. 'Me,' he says, 'I love James Blunt. I heard one of his songs on the radio. I don't know what it was, but something, something in it made me go out and buy the album. And fair play, it's one of the best albums I've ever heard.' This example alone proves he's failed to register my line of reasoning. James Blunt's debut single, 'You're Beautiful', holds the number one position in the current British charts, a feckless piano ballad, the lyrics consisting principally of the words *You're beautiful*. Amongst the rock fraternity it's earned the artist the moniker of James Cunt. I don't mean to come across as a culture snob but the sheer number of people I encounter in the Valleys who are

189

ignorant to musical and artistic diversity never ceases to amaze me. When a stranger asks me what I do for a living and I reveal that I'm a writer, nine times out of ten their response is, 'Romance novels, is it?' Pretty soon, you stop giving people the benefit of the doubt and start assuming that they're stupid – gormless shells, spoon-fed by consumerism. We only entered into the conversation because on arrival he'd gawped at my fishnet stockings and motorbike boots and said, 'It must be some sort of Goth band you're going to see.'

Raindrops begin to hit the windows as we drive across the Rhigos, a murder of crows circling in the grey sky above us. As we drop down into Hirwaun, we pass the Tower Colliery, the only place in Wales where winding gear is still used to take working miners, rather than tourists, underground.

'Anyway,' the taxi driver says, 'this band. It only takes a snapshot moment for their fortune to change, to be on the right stage with the right person in the audience, just one person who believes in them and who has the sway to make them. One moment and it *could* happen.' For once I think – I hope – he could be onto something.

Another Wetherspoons, another town. We're in Aberdare, just across the road from Blacks, where Midasuno are going to play the last show of their summer tour. They'll be supported by The Next Nine Years and Pete's Sake who are playing their very last gig before formally handing guitarist Ryan over to the headliners. Gavin is in the No Smoking area eating a meal with Rachel, his girlfriend. The table is crammed with bowls of mashed potato, Lincolnshire sausages standing up in the onion gravy like fat brown fingers. I'm waiting for the barmaid to measure our double vodkas, fretting in the mirror over my unwashed hair, when I see Gavin raise his hand to beckon us.

Darran and I carry our cans of Red Bull to the adjacent table before all the other band members begin arriving with their own girlfriends, swathes of polka dot, leopard skin and black and white check, black lace, black denim, black hair. This is the rock 'n' roll equivalent of an office Christmas party; the end of tour knees-up. I feel ill at ease being in such close proximity to the band while they go about their private lives. Lester Bang's chief advice to all aspiring music journalists was to avoid becoming friends with musicians because friendship impairs impartiality. Matt, who's still adhering to the terms of his diet, sips from a pint of tap water, telling me he has the post-tour sulk even before the tour has officially ended. The mere smell of sheep shit from Dowlais Mountain on their journey home last night depressed him. Lyndon was voted Prick of the Day. He has some kind of prick gene in him, Matt says. Tomorrow, when the rest of the band are in their beds nursing hangovers, he's going on eBay with the swag bag of MP3 players and digital cameras left on the tour bus by overwrought and drunken fans.

Blacks was until very recently The Black Lion, a traditional spit and sawdust pub with a wood burning fire in the centre of the lounge. Locals once spotted Johnny Depp drinking in there. He was filming on location in Monmouth but during one of his breaks hired a Ford Sierra and took a leisurely drive with his wife Vanessa Paradis into the Valleys for a pint of beer. Now it's a night club and live venue, its interior walls painted crimson, flanked by blue UV lights. The letters missing from its new name have left a dark imprint of the word 'Lion' on the fawn-coloured façade of the building. We're on the street outside taking photographs of Scott hugging his girlfriend. There's a queue for the club reaching across the square, Beth amongst it. 'Can you move forward a bit, Siân?' Darran says, summoning Scott's girlfriend closer.

'This isn't Siân,' Scott says. 'This is Lorne.'

We stand looking at them bewilderedly for a moment. Darran has picked the name Siân up from listening subconsciously to me. That was the name of the girlfriend with whom he split up. Given that it only happened in April, I assumed they'd got back together. Three months wouldn't give him sufficient time to find a new beau. But obviously it has, being the lead singer of Midasuno and everything.

'Sorry,' I say, 'I thought you were Siân.' It's evidence at least that I haven't got all *that* friendly with the band.

'I'm Lorne,' she says.

'It's okay,' Scott says. 'She knows everything. I tell her everything that happens on tour. She's seen the tour brief. "Anything off the record, say off the record." There is no off the record, is there?' Not for Scott, no. He gets slightly more protective during the gig when his younger brother and The Next Nine Years' bass player, after colliding several times, square up to one another on the dance floor, the result of the highly energetic and jostling crowd. 'Any fucker wants to have a go at him,' Scott says, speaking into the microphone, he points his brother out, 'they have to come through me.' That established, the party spills gleefully into Sunday.

September 10th 2005: a mild Saturday evening, the streets of Newport town centre alive with weekenders; half-cut couples, the women in cropped white gypsy skirts and sandals, and the men in Welsh rugby shirts, screaming obscenities at each other as they pass. We're standing in a queue the length of Clarence Place, amongst mobs of punks; people who have been punks since the genre emerged in 1976, green and pink luminescent Mohicans stiffened with flour and water, black leather biker jackets hemmed with studs, eighteen-eyelet Dr Martens, safety pins in their earlobes and nostrils, tartan bondage trousers, the lot. Less visible are the punk pop, nu-metal and emo kids, wearing cropped jeans and key chains, baseball caps, skate trainers, girls in tutu skirts and leggings à la Avril Lavigne and eighties Madonna. They could learn a thing or two from their elders were they not glued to their phone screens; typing text messages bound for their entire social circle about the topping of the pizza they ate last night.

'Get your ID ready,' the doorman shouts, ripping tickets in two and pocketing one half. Ryan comes out of the club and spots me in the queue. He can't understand why the crowd isn't filtering in any faster. It's almost empty inside and Midasuno are due onstage in ten minutes. Most of their fans are still stuck in the tailback.

Inside the venue Scott is nervous as hell. He stands chatting to Dan, his shoulders hunched, his eyes popping out of his face. He looks for a moment as if he's staring at me but he's gazing into the middle distance, blinded by his own trepidation. I haven't been in contact with anyone from the band since the end of the tour last month. News was they all swore a fortnight on the wagon, suffering as they were with severe withdrawal symptoms. But now is not the time to go and catch up. They have their own area at the back of the club, next to the backstage door. Gavin and Rachel are locked in a pre-gig clinch. Matt sits on the tan leather bench drumming the empty seat beside him. They're already dressed in their suits, red eye-shadow daubed in their eye sockets. Even Gavin is wearing make-up, proof if nothing else, that this is a

193

particularly significant show. Behind me, the punters begin trickling in, fastening the red and white striped arm bands to their wrists, queuing again at the bar.

This is TJ's, Britain's closest entity to New York City's CBGB's; an unlikely cultural landmark, famous for its shitty lavatories, shitty décor, shitty location and its reputation for wonderfully original underground rock music. Punk rock folklore has it that this is where Kurt Cobain proposed to Courtney Love – Hole in their very early days completing a British toilet circuit tour, the frontwoman's boyfriend hooking up with her at the tail end, a pink heart-shaped box full of coins and trinkets and coloured marbles in his pocket, the lid held on with a rubber band. He probably thought they were still in England. To the chagrin of legions of female Kurt Cobain fans, Love accepted of course. The rest is notorious. My favourite thread of this tale is that when Cobain tried to cross the club threshold, entrance fee unsettled, the doorman reprimanded him. 'Do you know who I am? I'm Kurt Cobain, the frontman of Nirvana.' I don't care who you are, the doorman said, it costs three pounds to get in. Cobain paid. It's also the location of the commencement of Cool Cymru. Long before Branson got wind of the Stereophonics, the ink on the statements in the Richey Edwards missing person's enquiry still wet (the last sighting was at the local bus station ironically), the club was full of London A&R scouring the dilapidated area for the musical equivalent of Kate Moss's heroin chic – signalling minor successes for the 60ft Dolls and the Big Leaves. 'The Legendary TJ's' is legendary, but made less so by the inclusion of the axiom in its new name.

Midasuno take the stage, all six of them, resolute. The audience crowds from the front of the stage to the wall on the opposite side of the club. I'm standing at the back, listening intently to the set. They only have six songs to impress the hardcore punk element. Second up is 'The Law of Tooth and Fang'. Since the end of the tour I've been hankering to hear it again, it's a catchy little bastard, annoying since I don't have it on CD. It's Scott's personal paean to Hunter S Thompson, someone with whom he likes to think he shares his outlaw-esque ways. Thompson's taste for the peculiar had a massive impact on him when he watched *Fear and Loathing in Las Vegas*, way back in 2002. Then he went out and bought the back catalogue. On tour he told me *The Rum Diary* was being scripted for film.

'Hunter S Thompson always stood on the wrong side of the tracks,' he said, 'knew his position and thoroughly believed his word was the gospel and the right thing to believe in. We recognised his attitude and made an instant kinship. We have to fight to do what we know is right in our heart. South Wales has been revered for good music but has also spawned an unbelievable number of wannabes and hangers-on. We have to wade through this and without the spirit of the outsider we wouldn't float above the corpses of the bands who are just in it for the moment.' Defiance, it just won't go away. They close the set with 'Start the Riot'. Everyone who I can see from where I'm standing is shouting the lyrics back at the band. Familiar faces, not only from previous Midasuno gigs but from my hometown of Treorchy. The Misfits visiting Britain is a major event and enthusiasts from all over South Wales have made the pilgrimage. Supporting them is no trifling feat but it stops short of a full tour. Everybody here already knows the music of Midasuno. What the band would benefit from is a chance to accumulate fans in new vicinities. For tonight though, their job is done, as well as it can be. One of

Midasuno's close friends, a thickset blond who always turns up to their gigs in outlandish fancy dress (tonight he's wearing a pink rugby jersey, one of a batch that belonged once to a holidaying hen party, the bold black characters printed across the shoulders spelling the Christian name Sharon), shows his appreciation by diving from the side of the stage, slipping in a spilt pint of cider and eventually careering into the cigarette machine. The aftershow party is just getting started when I whip the felt tip setlist from Dan's hand. I duck out to the front of the venue and watch the Misfits gig on a portable television next to the merchandise stand with Beth. Funny to think that they're closer to fifty than twenty, but their skin is still smudged with skeletal face-paint. Funny to think it's Dez Cadena up there playing guitar, the original guitarist in Black Flag, the singer of which was Henry Rollins, the man who made me want to start writing about rock music in the first place: the invisible roads of influence plotted on indiscernible maps, crossing through continents, generations, psyches...

Scott and Matt are leaning on the wrought iron railings of the balcony, the steel fire exit behind them ajar, daubs of grey clashing against the red brick of the Pop Factory. The sun is going down behind the third storey.

'Our bass player's late,' Scott says, sucking air over his teeth. 'This is another thing for your book; if he doesn't turn up, we're going to sack him.' Gavin is doing extra work for the new BBC Wales production of *Dr Who*, held up in Cardiff by the Friday rush hour traffic. 'We've tried to sack him before, you know,' Scott says, his hand shielding his eyes as he looks out over Porth, like a pirate surveying a target. The sound department have refused to supply Midasuno with adequate equipment, which means transporting their own kit from Merthyr to the Rhondda in various people's cars. Black Betty is leased out on another band's tour and the smaller vehicles, cheap adolescent run-arounds with rusting wheel arches and novelty air fresheners, line up on the forecourt beside Stuart Cable's yellow New York taxi (a prop from an old television series in which Cable drove around Wales, interviewing Welsh celebrities). The security guards crowd menacingly at the entrance in their black bomber jackets. Two members of Along Came Man stand amongst them, staring suspiciously at us. I approach the posse, explaining that this is *my* book launch, *my* party, but they won't let me in the venue while I'm carrying a box of Corona and a giant bottle of Jack Daniels. Only alcohol bought on the premises is allowed to be consumed inside the building. The rider with which I'm paying the band to perform at my own function prevents my admittance. If I'd wanted trimmings I should have paid the Pop Factory to supply them, so Matt loads the alcohol onto the back seat of his father's car.

The wallpaper pasting table in the corner of the television studio is laden with copies of my new book *Fresh Apples*, alongside a wooden basket of pallid Granny Smiths. I'm proud of the sickly psychedelic yellow dust jacket, a Jo Mazelis photograph of a pound of apples and a doll, stuffed into a polythene bag. The doll is one of those sinister types; crochet dress and blinking eyelids. I've been carrying a copy around on me since it got printed at the end of August. I know the blurb on the back by heart:

> Johnny Mental was sitting on his porch wearing sunglasses, drinking lager, his teeth orange and ugly. Someone was painting their front door a few yards away, with a portable

197

radio playing soul music; Diana Ross or some shit. A big burgundy Vauxhall Cavalier came around the corner, real slow like an old man on a hill.

It's an extract from the title story, about a sixteen-year-old boy who's getting peer pressure to lose his virginity so he tries it on with his friend's Down's syndrome sister, and then he tries to throw himself under a train. I took the idea from Kurt Cobain's posthumously published diary and implanted it into the Rhondda. Lyndon and Chris are flicking through the pages when Chris looks up suddenly. 'Have you heard of Johnny Mental then?' he says. The Johnny Mental he's referring to is a local rock band. The Johnny Mental I was referring to when I wrote the story was a notorious drug addict and small time dealer from the immediate vicinity who died, like Jimi Hendrix, from choking on his own vomit. 'Yes,' I say, avoiding a garrulous explanation. 'Cool!' he says. Midasuno are not particularly competitive. In fact they are great supporters of many of their contemporaries including the Cardiff-based Panel and The Next Nine Years, who they took on tour earlier this year. An exception it seems is Bullet for My Valentine. They're making jokes about them, snarling through their laughter. Two days ago, *Kerrang!* plucked this band, presumably from its own arse, and slapped them on its cover, hailing them as neo-British metal superstars. Ahead of this event, nobody had actually heard of them. On closer inspection it turned out they were originally Jeff Killed John, a Bridgend four-piece who had yet to venture out of Bridgend and who earned their crumbs playing Metallica and Maiden covers. How they leapt from this guise, so swiftly and seamlessly into the 'Gods' and 'heroes' they're being described as, is an impenetrable mystery. I'd assume it was a textbook example of sour grapes on Midasuno's part if I hadn't read the

198

article myself; a wholly infantile Q&A manufactured from musings about their favourite cock films, their preferred method of masturbation and their bassist's fondness for writing 'bummer' on his band mates' foreheads when they're asleep, puerility laid on extra thick. It's condescending almost to the point of hoax. I'm well aware that rock music is for the most part the domain of miscreant males, but does that mean it has to be mindless and juvenile?

When my publisher arrives, I quickly remember why I'm here. Standing on a stage reading extracts of my prose to total strangers is never a nerveless chore but this is getting a little thicker than usual. Most people here are kids who have come to see Midasuno. Given the aforementioned style of current rock journalism, guitar music and literature blend together like oil and water. I go down to the forecourt where Ryan and Lyndon have arranged an assembly of metal chairs on which to drink their whiskey, just out of view of the churlish bouncers. I suck from the rim of the bottle like there's no future, shivering in my wrap-around dress. It's the middle of September and winter has just landed. Two hours slip away while I summon Dutch courage. Come show time, I can't actually see who's in the hall but I know it's full because it's dense with conversation. I step up onto the stage, somehow overcoming my earlier fear of falling arse over tit and mutter something about knowing everyone's only here for the band, stretching to reach Chris' microphone. He looks short in real life. How come his mic towers above me? Straight into the first line: 'When you get oil from a locomotive engine all over the arse of your best blue jeans, it looks like shit: black and sticky.' *Shit* gets a giggle, so I decide I might be alright. Scott appears before me and readjusts the microphone stand before walking backwards to his position in front of the stage. All of the Midasuno boys are there listening intently. The rest of it is plain sailing; aided by the fact my protagonist is a Metallica fan who wants to play drums like Tommy Lee. There's a raucous cry of approval every time I drop a 'fuck'. When the whispers of conversation start at the bar Scott puts his finger to lips. 'Sssshhhh,' he says, frowning. I step off the stage to a round of applause and the opening riff of Mötley Crüe's 'Live Wire', having roped Emily in to DJ for the night. Scott is waiting with a pint of lager, bought for me by his ex-girlfriend Siân. I return briefly to the temporary beer garden on the forecourt and vomit a bucket load of ginger saccharine stinking bile onto the smashed concrete floor, my friend Lisa rubbing my back, my chest held in my flimsy dress by two strips of double-sided parcel adhesive posing as tit tape. When I get back to the book sale table to do signatures I try to rearrange my wrap-around dress, untying the belt, whipping it open to my bare body and retying it to sit properly on my disproportionate child-bearing hips, as I had done a thousand times in the floor to ceiling mirror before I left the house, oblivious suddenly to the crowds of people around me. My last memory of the evening is standing bowed towards Scott in the centre of the empty room, both of us talking tripe at one another, froth dribbling down my chin. He reaches into his jean pocket and toys something out, passing it to me in his clenched fist. When I look down into my palm I see it's a plectrum, one side printed with a diagram of a woman's midriff, a woman in blue jeans. On the flipside there's a diagram of the same woman's posterior, a red thong riding up the small of her back.

This is the End

Eight months after I began following Midasuno around the country like a brooding ewe, I'm back where the expedition commenced. It's 8pm Sunday, 20th November. The Womanby Street lane is pitch black, lit only at either end by the Christmas lights nailed to the wall of Cardiff Castle, and the yellow glow from the front door of the Gatekeeper pub. The sky above is clear, the stars glimmering against the night. Beneath my khaki blazer I'm wearing a thin Midasuno T-shirt, the *Til Death Do Us Party* logo propped under a film reel featuring an assortment of women's faces, captured amid throes of ecstasy, the images already blistered by wash cycles. Clwb Ifor Bach is in danger of violating its capacity and is operating a one out, one in policy. I send Emily up to the auditorium and wait in the foyer for someone to leave, my black and white striped scarf coiled around the lower half of my face, the doorman engrossed in a Niall Griffiths paperback. Earlier in the day I'd eaten my roast chicken dinner whilst listening to a Radio Wales programme about myself, perched on the edge of the settee, mortified by my own Rhondda Valley accent. At various intervals in the interview, the programme cut to minor snippets of dialogue from my contemporaries; other writers talking about my work. The final guest was Scott, his silver media tongue working its customary magic:

I think even though the Valleys are quite grim and a lot of people who can put up with mundanity actually create a fairytale world for themselves.

'Go on,' the doorman says without looking up from his book. 'You've waited long enough.' He gestures with his chin to the plastic ring-punched armbands sitting in a small pile on the counter. I pick one and carry it up the steel stairs with me. Emily is waiting on the landing and we push into the top floor hall. It's crammed with Midasuno fans in their signature leopard skin and polka dots, musky and hot. Many people are already lined up in front of the stage, waiting for the band to emerge. While I'm observing this spectacle, a bottle of beer to my face, I notice a girl with a big tattoo on her chest.

On Saturday, 3rd September 2005, Hanah Heath, a geography student from the University of Glamorgan in Pontypridd, walked into John Treharne's Cardiff tattoo parlour and asked for the word **MIDASUNO** to be written in inch high black block lettering, four centimetres under her left clavicle bone, which is exactly what she got. The word jumps out from beneath the strap of her polka dot blouse, still scabby and swollen.

'It's directly above my heart,' she says, 'which is where the boys from Midasuno are; in my heart.' Most signed bands need to verify their longevity with a succession of albums before one of their ardent fans does something as passionate as this. Midasuno have managed this exploit even without a record deal. I smile supportively at the student. I'm a great believer in any kind of body modification which sets people apart as individuals, as opposed to the kind of body modification which turns people into clones: tit jobs and nose jobs *et al*, but what makes this encounter slightly awkward is the recent news announcing Midasuno are about to change their name. Rumours that they were splitting began to surface when their website billed this show as their penultimate. Fans left frantic messages demanding to know what it meant exactly. Scott eventually wrote a blog on the band's myspace site revealing the band intended to change its moniker in order to accommodate Ryan, Lyndon and Chris, the three members who joined the ensemble long since the original name was coined. The new name is still strictly secret; to be revealed following their final gig as Midasuno next month, but there's much speculation on the grapevine about 'The Suicide Family'. 'What will you do?' I ask with much consternation, 'when they divulge their new name?' Hanah seems undaunted. 'I'll get that one tattooed on the other side.'

The band unsurprisingly play a blinder. At the end of the set Scott invites the audience onto the stage, a repeat performance of the madcap display I'd seen earlier in Yeovil. For a moment nobody moves from where they're standing, presumably wondering if they heard his summons right. My friend Lisa says, 'Go on, go up there Rach,' pointing at the stage encouragingly. I'm deterred by the quandary of what to do when I actually get there. 'C'mon,' Scott says, 'what's the difference between you and me? Nothing, come on up here, you're all stars.' His request is an echo from a phone conversation we had recently in which he said, 'I'm

203

not doing anything that some other kid couldn't do if he put his fucking mind and bollocks into it.' Scott is very clearly contemplating his appeal as a performer and has come up with an astute way of making himself simultaneously both accessible, and unobtainable. He is rewarding those tasteful enough to admire him with the very thing they want, what everybody wants – to momentarily, if not perpetually, be the centre of all attention. It's a perfect circle of fandom working in perfect rotation, whether he realises it or not. Within a minute, half of the audience is up there, jumping, dancing, shouting, shaking Scott's hand, ruffling his hair. Someone produces a can of silly string and squirts it onto the stage, the yellow, foamy cable encasing band and fans together in a spider web of fleeting unity.

As I'm shuffling out of the auditorium, small tiptoe steps, my body flanked by a file of people doing exactly the same thing, Gavin is shuffling in to collect more gear, a soft leather biker jacket draped over his shoulders. 'Hiya Rach.' The words are actually inaudible. He simply mouths them but I hear. We squeeze past one another, upper arm to upper arm, all broad smiles. When he's gone, when he's on the stage coiling his bass wire and I'm on the metal stairs on my way out of the club, I can still see him smiling. My mind's eye has captured the image and it continues to play repeatedly like a kaleidoscopic film; Gavin getting closer, closer, touching, going, gone. Closer, closer, touching, going, gone. 'Don't they *look* like a band?' Emily says, startling me. 'My favourite thing when I go to a gig is watching how the people around me react. There was a bloke standing next to me, he looked like a maths teacher; he knew every word. And that little guitarist! Phwoar!' She pushes her debit card into the car park ticket machine.

'That's Chris,' I say, 'he's only, like, twelve.'

One of the security guards on the front door has a beast of a black eye; his eyeball crimson where it should be white, the lids around it bloated and purple. The doorwoman is a sturdy, no nonsense, peroxide blonde. They stand at the top of the staircase leading into the building; an old 1950s picture house built with colliers' proceeds, slap in the middle of Merthyr town centre. It's been very loosely 'converted' into a club called The Studio Bar; a gigantic incandescent coloured poster pasted to its façade announces Midasuno's last gig. Inside, the walls are still plastered with framed photographs of Marilyn Monroe, Audrey Hepburn and Marlon Brando, along with more recent movie posters advertising *Rocky IV* and *The Silence of the Lambs*; their dog-eared corners lurching away from their globs of Blu-tack. The vast auditorium has been messily divided into three sections. There's a pool hall where a gang of teenagers in tracksuits measure up their shots, their fingers hidden behind gold sovereign rings. The billiard tables are covered in blue felt. The balls are the American-style multicoloured dots and stripes. Adjoined to it is a row of fast food restaurant style tables, the orange chairs fixed to the ground. The stage is five foot high, the surrounding walls hand painted with cartoon movie reels. It says NEW YORK on one side, HOLLYWOOD on the other, and given that it's December, gaunt rows of tinsel loop across the ceiling. The bar and the hot-dog hut stand next to one another on the pine-end wall, a gummy strip of red carpet leading towards it. It's positively glacial. I've been standing in the queue for over a minute and I can still see the frost in my breath. Scott's description of the place was spot on. 'Imagine *Grease*,' he said, 'set in the heart of the Gurnos.'

Straight on the vodka and Red Bull. It's not actually Red Bull, but an even sweeter imitation. One of the support bands are on the stage making a holy racket. Gavin is standing on the middle of the dance floor with his hoody pulled up over his head, watching them intently. The lead singer knows him. He keeps interrupting his own songs to inform the entire room of their acquaintance, saying, 'Jessop, boy!' or 'This one's for you, Jess.' It's been a fortnight and I've thought about him a lot. His peculiar allure originates, I know, from a mixture of circumstance and misguided emotion. A) I'm marrying Darran in twelve months time and regardless of my longing to do just that, the closer the date creeps, the jitterier I become about finally parting with my sexual liberty. B) I often do get strangely attracted to men who are for the most part ineffectual but who disguise it commendably with bravado and a forged veneer of sang-froid. C) I have a deluded desire to execute the initial objective of this exercise, which was to make Justin Hawkins fall in love with me. Justin Hawkins is long gone, of course, and Gavin doesn't have his money, or even the capability of falling in love. He has a girlfriend of his own for one thing, although flirt shamelessly with me on tour, he did. This compulsion is futile, something I'm well aware of in sobriety but I'm on my third double now and the devil always makes work for cold and idle hands.

'Give it up for Midasuno,' the lead singer says. 'They're coming on next now, and I just want to say Merthyr's not going to be the same without them. They've been a massive influence on me like, and probably everyone else here.'

It's sweaty down the front, a veritable mosh-pit; kids leaping into one another, throwing each other around and trying to kick my feet from underneath me. I have to hold onto the lip of the stage to make sure I'm not caught up in it. Beth is behind me, dancing with a tall, scrawny guy in a titfer hat. Scott's swinging his microphone around like a golf club, its rubber-tipped legs in the air. As it's their last gig, they've pulled out all the stops, which means playing their very early material for a final time, 'The Art of Fear' and 'Cut Ribbons'. They even do 'Hypocrite'. Goose pimples prickle my forearms when the drums pause for Scott to utter the first breathy lines. 'Nothing meant that much to me. A chasm filled in time, I'm losing touch.' I'm standing directly underneath Gavin and I reach up to feel his calves through the abrasive polyester of his moss-green trousers. Sentiment is running high. It's the end of the book, the end of Midasuno and the end of the year. It's the last gathering of all these people after all that tightly-packed time of travel. It doesn't seem like it's over though. Just hitting its stride.

As I'm making to leave, already embarrassed by the leg thing, I see a disposable lighter on the floor. It's full of gas, I can see it through the transparent case, so I bend to pick it up and pocket it. When I stand again, Gavin's in front of me. 'You were great tonight,' he says. I look at him for a moment, trying to decipher this ambiguous comment. 'I was great?' I say, pointing at myself disbelievingly. '*You* were great.' He opens his arms, inviting a goodbye cuddle. Outside, my taxi's waiting. The driver has ventured into the foyer to look for me. 'Are you Rachel?' the doorwoman asks. When I concur, following the driver out into the street, she puts her finger into the air as though she's going to say something else, but then forgets it and turns away. We indicate out of the High Street, the ostentatious Christmas lights strung from the telegraph poles fading to blips in the back windscreen. I'm dying for a piss already but I cross my legs and hold tight. I'm only half an hour away from home.

207

Afterword

E. Booth heard the solemn whisper of the god of all arts. 'I shall give you hunger and pain and sleepless nights, also beauty and satisfaction known to few, and glimpses of the heavenly life. None of these you shall have continually, and of their coming and going you shall not be foretold.'

The Players Club, *Edward Booth's Legacy*

It's the 26th of June 2006, and Nelly Furtado's 'Maneater' has been number one in the UK single chart for several weeks. She and her record producer Timbaland listened constantly to 1980s pop music while holed up together, co-writing her forthcoming album. The result is a song which sounds *so* 1980s; people keep asking me if it's a sample. Somewhere beneath the layers of keyboard and drum effects they think they can hear Madonna or Blondie or Annie Lennox. Away from the mainstream, rock music too has adopted a taste for keyboard-driven melodies. AFI released their seventh studio album *December Underground* earlier this month, a veritable tribute to The Cure. New Cardiff indie band The Automatic look set to soar with their electro-emo debut album *Not Accepted Anywhere*. It sounds like I'm seven years old again, synthesizer beats marking my growing pains. I'll be twenty-eight in one week.

Six months have passed since I left Midasuno in the Studio Bar in Merthyr, surrounded by dusty Christmas trimmings and the smell of stale sweat and lager, their hands clamped around post-gig bottles of Budweiser, their fans pleading for a sneak preview of their new name. It feels like a lifetime ago. Today it's a humid Monday afternoon. I'm in the truck, on my way to meet Scott in Pontypridd. The weekend heat has given way to a cloying rainstorm, the customary pattern of the British summer. The sky is the colour of milk. Beads of rain beat infrequently on the windscreen while I wait in the traffic on Llantrisant common. There's a text message saying he's arrived at the bus station. 'Be there in five, lady!'

When I leave the Graig, approaching the town centre, I can see him standing in front of the derelict pub on the corner in his standard black clothing. That pub used to be Flicks, a rock nightclub. I'd never been there but I remember as a child watching the women in zebra print leggings loitering in the doorway. Since then it's been Silks, a dance nightclub. Its time-honoured moss-green tiles remain intact but inside it's empty. As I get closer I can see Scott's wearing a black beanie hat. Threads of his jet black hair fire out at the sides. He's carrying a big canvas shoulder bag. Under his lower eyelids there's a vague hint of pink eye-shadow but no dark bags.

'Wetherspoons is closed,' he says. 'Shall we go in here?' I turn into the Greyhound, an old sawdust pub which has recently been renovated to cater for middle-aged singletons, slightly dismayed that the Tumble Inn, the pub in which every interview I've conducted for this book, will not be the setting for the final one. The old framed pictures of local boxing champions have been cleaned up and put back on the freshly painted walls. I scan them while I wait for the barmaid to take a phone call from Spain. Scott is on his way home from Swansea where he spent the weekend with his girlfriend. He has a healthy air of alacrity about him, as though he has more important things to do elsewhere. This project has been ongoing for sixteen months. If it were a child it'd be walking by now. We both want to move on.

'I'll have a glass of water,' he says when the barmaid eventually tends to us. We sit on a fat brown leather settee in a murky corner of the pub, creased manilla envelopes containing assorted drafts of the book scattered on the coffee table in front of us. A man on the adjacent table, seemingly amused by Scott's appearance, folds his tabloid newspaper away and blatantly begins to listen to our conversation. Scott picks up where we left off.

The thing about Midasuno's last gig at the Studio Bar, he says, was that it wasn't Midasuno's last gig, not really. Long before they'd decided to change their name they'd been booked to play a New Year's Eve show at Flicks in Yeovil. Contractually bound, they had to go ahead with it. Instead of advertising it in the usual way, they kept the gig a near secret, only inviting friends and family; a private party in effect. John drove the bus of band members, girlfriends and friends to the venue, and as usual, most of them were full of vodka before they crossed the Severn Bridge. An hour before the band were due on stage, Scott was busy unloading gear when a drunken punter allegedly spat in Scott's girlfriend's face. Gavin spotted the altercation and moved in, asking Scott's distressed girlfriend what the problem was. In a bid to conceal the dispute from Scott and his volatile temper, Gavin approached the perpetrator himself, a feeble teenager, unable to handle his drink. Gavin lifted him from the floor and invited him to spit in *his* face. The boy mumbled a quivering apology and ran away. In the midst of the commotion however, Scott had worked out what was happening. He stormed out of the venue in search of the fugitive boy. Gavin then pursued Scott and when he reached him, spent fifteen minutes trying to assure him that the problem had been dealt with. There was nothing more anyone could do and they had half an hour until show time. Convinced that Scott had calmed down, Gavin walked him back to the venue. In the corridor leading towards the stage, they were placidly chatting about something completely unrelated to the incident when Scott noticed a vacuum cleaner plugged into a socket in the corner. He picked the cleaner up, pulling it free from the wall, and threw it with all his strength at a window on the other side of the corridor, instantly shattering it. One of the windowpanes undamaged, Scott then launched himself across the passage and into the glass. Gavin, holding him in an attempt to prevent any further damage, was slashed across the stomach by one of the vast flying shards. There was a vicious and prolonged struggle until security arrived and ushered Scott out of the building.

The band attempted to play without Scott, Chris striving to remember the lyrics and sing them whilst playing lead guitar. When the crowd began heckling, he apologised, explaining his lead singer had just been arrested. The derision increased, the audience taking his comment as a badly thought up joke. The setlist lasted one song, after which Matt punched the wall, snapping his wrist in the process. Scott Andrews is banned from Flicks in Yeovil for the rest of his life, which pretty much means Midasuno are too.

In January 2006 Ryan Day left the band. The Yeovil show was his last. He'd been a fan of Midasuno since they met on the local music circuit six years earlier, and had been *in* the band for six months. Being a fan of the band, he concluded, was a far more enjoyable experience than being in it. Now he had other interests to pursue. With one man down, the injured band members paused to take stock of their situation. Their fans were waiting for a new album and a new name, two things they were meant to release early in the New Year, but neither had been completed. The monikers the band was secretly considering were *Fire, Theft & Boom* and *The Suicide Family*. The album, after eleven months in the making, was almost finished, but not quite. A few of the songs on there were not strong enough to make the cut. The band decided to scrap the album for the moment, and still unsure about a definitive new name, continue temporarily as Midasuno. Everything the band had been working towards since their split with Lockjaw Records seemed to have ended in futility. I remember seeing Matt and Scott around this time at a Crimea gig in Cardiff. I was sitting in a pub a few yards from the venue when I heard a girl on a nearby table say to her friend, 'It's that boy from Midasuno, look.' When I looked up Scott was standing in front of me. I asked him how the band was doing. He told me they were due to play a series of secret gigs, all under different names. That seemed like a tremendously pointless exercise. I didn't know then that Ryan had left the band but I was sure they were hiding something from me, something ominous. There was still a lot of chat room speculation about their name. Their fans were becoming impatient. 'You have to tell *me*,' I said. 'I'm writing a book about you.'

'Well what it's going to be,' Scott said, 'is a text message about half an hour before the gig,' and he rushed off to the railway station to meet his girlfriend. I half expected the band to fade slowly into anonymity. Their former doggedness had melted into disinterest.

Indeed Scott began performing solo gigs, playing acoustic versions of Midasuno's material in the long established tradition of exasperated frontman jumping ship. This didn't last too long however. In February, only a month later, he came up with the idea of an EP. Four or five of the album tracks were exceptional compositions including 'A Machine; The Rhythm Thief' which appeared as a demo version on *Rock Sound* magazine's monthly compilation and bagged the best track vote. By taking the best of the album and shortening it to an EP, the band could still re-launch themselves, albeit on a slightly smaller scale, condensing the recording experience into a more urgent and immediate sounding release. The complete track listing would be: 'A Machine; The Rhythm Thief', 'The Law of Tooth and Fang', 'Taste The Virus', 'Shock Horror' and 'Sirens'. Excited by this initiative, Scott began work on new material. If the EP was successful then they'd still need to follow it up with an album. The tracks which had been dropped or used exclusively for the EP would need to be replaced. Any existing material not resilient enough to make the cut could be kept for B-sides. Some of them were already being played regularly on indie pirate radio stations. Scott was energised again by the thought of Midasuno's prospects. For the first time since Ryan had joined the previous July, the band began rehearsing in anticipation of their comeback gigs. To face the public however, the band needed a convincing name. They were still unsure about the two titles on the table. Ryan's departure had retained the original band line-up who had all been happy with the original name, so suddenly there seemed little purpose in changing it. The band had a raft of fans that had grown up with the title, including one who had it tattooed on her chest. 'Midasuno' was here to stay. Without further ado, the band began pursuing record labels through which to release the EP.

In April, Bristol-based independent company Sugar Shack Records offered them a deal. Against the never-ending wave of simpering, uninspired emo earsores and identikit New York via Camden indie soundalikes Midasuno will return with their EP *Til Death Do Us Party*, reminding people of the true meaning of 'alternative'. Their first release in almost three years, it's a stunning statement of intent – a massive aural 'fuck you and thank you' to the forces that have surrounded the band's seemingly ever fateful campaign to stay afloat in rock music's current climate whilst dignity and integrity remain intact.

When our formal interview is complete, Scott and I fall into a casual conversation about Guns 'n' Roses, our favourite subject matter. In 1994, after sustained alcohol and drug abuse, bassist Duff McKagan's pancreas exploded. Close to death, he quickly turned sober. In 2002 he set up supergroup Velvet Revolver with former Guns 'n' Roses guitarist Slash and drummer Matt Sorum. Former Stone Temple Pilots vocalist Scott Weiland joined them as frontman. Axl Rose is now the sole original member of Guns 'n' Roses. After ten years of near silence the band returned last month to play the UK's leading rock festival Download with former Nine Inch Nails guitarist

Robin Finck as part of its line-up. Scott says he's impressed by the early bootleg material he's heard. He even jokes about founding a Guns 'n' Roses tribute act. There's enough money in nostalgia to pay the bills of present-day. We conclude therefore, exactly where we began, because the end of Guns 'n' Roses is exactly where our shared obsession for authentic rock music started: Scott, ten years old and walking the streets of Troedyrhiw in cycling shorts and a bandana, me, a little older at fourteen, standing defiant in the school yard with my piercings and leather jacket. I set out on a very personal journey in search of the tenacious punk attitude that underlined the ethic of Guns 'n' Roses, one that would require the writing of the book itself to map and comprehend. Much of that mindset appears to be stunted by the end of socialism, the rise of communications, the rise of the idea of celebrity, a new found revulsion for the underdog. But there are sporadic exceptions and Midasuno are testament to that. The future, as ever, is uncertain, however. Scott hands me a bundle of flyers advertising the forthcoming release of the EP, hugs me and struts out of the pub. I turn to the man on the next table who has been listening throughout our discussion and I smile. He turns quickly away, affronted.

When I get home that evening, the house is empty save for the stifled murmurings of Radio One DJ Steve Lamacq. I leave the radio on while I prepare dinner. It's with absolute astonishment I hear him announce a band from Merthyr Tydfil called Midasuno. Disorientated, I rush into the living room and turn the radio up. It's playing Chris' opening chords to 'Rhythm Thief'. I turn it up again. Yeah, it's them, Midasuno, my Midasuno, on Radio bloody One.

ACKNOWLEDGEMENTS

Thanks are due to the following people who helped me work
on this book:

Scott Lee Andrews, Gwen Davies, Richard Davies, Ryan Day,
Darran Frowen, Lisa Hocking, Gavin Jessop, Lyndon Jones,
Lucy Llewellyn, Chris Morgan, John Riste, Matt Riste, Lloyd
Robson, Owen Sheers, Dominic Williams and Jeni Williams. I
am indebted to *Driving Home Both Ways*, an essay by Dylan
Moore from which I adapted the description of Merthyr in
Riding in Cars with Boys.

PARTHIAN

parthianbooks.co.uk

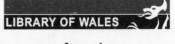

LIBRARY OF WALES

libraryofwales.org

Independent
Presses
Management
INPRESS

inpressbooks.co.uk

gwales.com
Llyfrau ar-lein
Books on-line

PARTHIAN

new writing

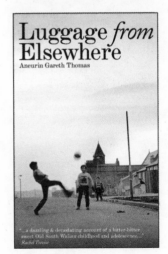

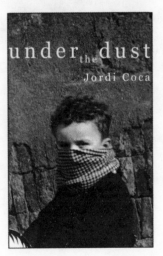

parthianbooks.co.uk